SCHOLASTIC

Fractured Fairy Tales Multiplication & Division

by Dan Greenberg

New York ❖ Toronto ❖ London ❖ Auckland ❖ Sydney
Mexico City ❖ New Delhi ❖ Hong Kong ❖ Buenos Aires

Teaching Resources

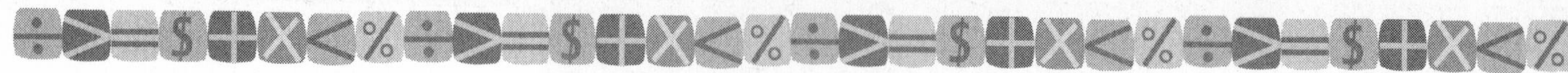

Cover design by Maria Lilja
Cover illustration by Doug Jones
Interior design by Kelli Thompson
Interior illustrations by Mike Moran

ISBN 0-439-51898-9

Printed in the U.S.A.

4 5 6 7 8 9 10 40 12 11 10 09 08

Contents

Contents

The 25 stories in *Fractured Fairy Tales: Multiplication & Division* all have a single purpose: to teach multiplication and division in an entertaining yet mathematically rigorous context. The stories themselves are based on familiar fairy tales, fables, and related concepts. However, they've all been transformed into something new and, we hope, very funny. For example, Humpty Dumpty appears as a TV talk show host, while Goldie Loxe is a food critic, and Beauty reveals the bittersweet experience of being married to a "beast" named Walter.

Each story serves as a launching pad into a key mathematical concept. The book begins by introducing multiplication and division as basic concepts, and uses visual examples to reinforce students' understanding of the material. From there, individual stories progress in skill level, moving through basic multiplication and division facts, to multi-digit multiplication, to long division, and finally to multiplication and division of fractions and decimals. Each story provides model problems for students to work through before they begin their own computation.

Simple word problems as well as more complex problem solving exercises are provided throughout the text, as well as special math topics such as interpreting remainders, solving multistep problems, finding perimeter and area, and using a calculator. Special emphasis in the book is placed on mental math and estimation, encouraging students to use these skills as checks for all kinds of calculations. You will find complete answer key that starts on page 60.

We recommend the following ways to use these activities in the classroom:

- Whole class participation, in which students or the teacher read the story aloud, solve one or more model problem examples, and then solve problems individually.
- Small group participation, in which 2 to 5 students work together to master the material.
- Individual participation, in which students read the stories and solve the problems on their own.

We encourage students to engage the stories directly by writing their own responses, comments, and/or questions to events that take place in the text. One fun, cross-curricular option might have students write their own "fractured" fairy tales to complement the stories that they have read.

Overall, the stories in this book are intended to appeal to all kinds of learners—including students not easily motivated by traditional textbooks—making math learning fun and accessible for all.

	Number and Operations	Algebra	Geometry	Measurement	Data Analysis and Probability	Problem Solving	Reasoning and Proof	Communication	Connections	Representation
The Humpty Dumpty Show	X					X	X	X	X	X
Goldie Loxe Jones, Famous Food Critic, Searches for the Best Porridge in America	X					X	X	X	X	X
The Lion and the Mouse	X			X	X	X	X	X	X	X
Turtle Gets a Makeover	X			X		X	X	X	X	X
How to Break Out of the Dungeon	X			X	X	X	X	X	X	X
I Married a Beast!	X			X		X	X	X	X	X
Interview With a Fool	X					X	X	X	X	X
Advice From Morris the Wise One	X			X		X	X	X	X	X
More Advice From Morris the Wise One	X			X		X	X	X	X	X
The Prime Minister's Dog	X					X	X	X	X	X
Medieval Monarch Magazine: For the Ruler Who Has Everything (and Wants More)	X					X	X	X	X	X
The Snake in the River	X			X		X	X	X	X	X
Channel F Presents: Happily Ever After	X					X	X	X	X	X
The Two Warthogs	X			X		X	X	X	X	X
Johnny Icarus and Ed Dedalus	X					X	X	X	X	X
The Magic Dancing Shoes	X			X		X	X	X	X	X
Jack and the Magic Beans, Part 1	X			X		X	X	X	X	X
Jack and the Magic Beans, Part 2	X			X		X	X	X	X	X
The Fisherman and His Fish	X			X		X	X	X	X	X
The Elves and the Screenwriter	X					X	X	X	X	X
King Vitas and the Fraction Touch	X					X	X	X	X	X
The Duck Puppy	X	X		X		X	X	X	X	X
The Leap Frogs	X		X	X		X	X	X	X	X
Modern Medieval Science Magazine	X			X		X	X	X	X	X
The Four Beautiful Ducklings	X			X	X	X	X	X	X	X

Name ______________________________ Date ______________

The Humpty Dumpty Show

Announcer: *LIVE from Fairy Land, it's the Humpty Dumpty Show, starring the world's biggest egg, Humpty Dumpty.*

Humpty: Hello, I'm Humpty Dumpty. I sat on a wall. I had a great fall. And now it's time to welcome my first guest, Little Bo Peep. How's it goin', Bo?

Peep: What's there to say, Humpty? I'm Little Bo Peep. I've lost my sheep. I don't know where to find them.

Humpty: That's tough, Bo. Really tough. Have you tried leaving them alone? I mean, isn't it likely that they'll come home, perhaps even wagging their tails behind them?

Peep: Leave them alone? You're joking! You know what happens when you leave sheep alone? They stay out all night, *BAA*-ing at things. I'm *sick* of it. I'm sick of sheep!

Humpty: I'm sorry to hear that, Bo. Perhaps we should take a break.

Model

How many sheep has Bo Peep lost?
To find out, you can multiply 3 groups of 4.

3 x 4 = 12 sheep

Multiply to find how many sheep there are.

1. 2 x 5 = ______ sheep

2. 3 x 6 = ______ sheep

3. 4 x 2 = ______ sheep

Humpty: Welcome back, folks. Now it's time to meet my next guest, the Old Woman Who Lives in a Shoe. Come in, Old Woman!

Woman: Come in yourself, you big Egg!

Humpty: Why the hard feelings, Old Woman?

Woman: I don't like being called the Old Woman Who Lives in a Shoe.

Humpty: But isn't that who you are?

Woman: Aren't you the Dumb Egg Who Fell Off a Wall?

Humpty: Well, yes, but—

Concept of Multiplication, Multiplication Facts

Name ______________________________ **Date** ______________

Woman: And, I don't *live* in a shoe. My name is Brenda and I work in a Kids Fun Center that happens to be *shaped* like a shoe. And I know what to do with my children. I just don't know how many I have because they keep moving around in different groups.

Here are some of the groups. Write a multiplication problem for each picture. Then find the product.

4. ______ x ______ = ______ children

5. ______ x ______ = ______ children

6. ______ x ______ = ______ children

Humpty: That's all the time we have, everybody. I'd like to thank my guests, Little Bo Peep and the Old Woman Who Lives in a Shoe.

Woman: I told you, my name is Brenda, not "Old Woman."

Humpty: Sorry. Good night Brenda. And good night, Bo.

Peep: G'night, Humpty. And as far as I'm concerned, if you see my sheep you can keep them, Humpty.

Humpty: This is Humpty Dumpty, saying: I sat on a wall. I had a great fall. Then all the king's horses and all the king's men—they couldn't put me back together again. Good night, everyone. I'll leave you with these multiplication problems while we roll the credits.

Multiply.

7. 7 x 3 = _______ king's men

8. 8 x 2 = _______ horses

9. 4 x 7 = _______ chicks

10. 7 x 4 = _______ eggs

Humpty: Join me next week when I'll ask my special guest, Mary, Mary Quite Contrary, this question: How does your garden grow?

THE END

Concept of Multiplication, Multiplication Facts

Name ______________________ Date ____________

Fill in the table.

1 x 1 =	1 x 2 =	1 x 3 =	1 x 4 =	1 x 5 =	1 x 6 =	1 x 7 =	1 x 8 =	1 x 9 =
2 x 1 =	2 x 2 =	2 x 3 =	2 x 4 =	2 x 5 =	2 x 6 =	2 x 7 =	2 x 8 =	2 x 9 =
3 x 1 =	3 x 2 =	3 x 3 =	3 x 4 =	3 x 5 =	3 x 6 =	3 x 7 =	3 x 8 =	3 x 9 =
4 x 1 =	4 x 2 =	4 x 3 =	4 x 4 =	4 x 5 =	4 x 6 =	4 x 7 =	4 x 8 =	4 x 9 =
5 x 1 =	5 x 2 =	5 x 3 =	5 x 4 =	5 x 5 =	5 x 6 =	5 x 7 =	5 x 8 =	5 x 9 =
6 x 1 =	6 x 2 =	6 x 3 =	6 x 4 =	6 x 5 =	6 x 6 =	6 x 7 =	6 x 8 =	6 x 9 =
7 x 1 =	7 x 2 =	7 x 3 =	7 x 4 =	7 x 5 =	7 x 6 =	7 x 7 =	7 x 8 =	7 x 9 =
8 x 1 =	8 x 2 =	8 x 3 =	8 x 4 =	8 x 5 =	8 x 6 =	8 x 7 =	8 x 8 =	8 x 9 =
9 x 1 =	9 x 2 =	9 x 3 =	9 x 4 =	9 x 5 =	9 x 6 =	9 x 7 =	9 x 8 =	9 x 9 =

Name ______________________________ Date ____________

Goldie Loxe Jones, Famous Food Critic, Searches for the Best Porridge in America

There was once a Famous Food Critic for a great metropolitan newspaper. That would be me—Goldie Loxe Jones. Not to toot my own horn, but I'm a very fine food critic.

But it wasn't always this way. At one point in my career, I was a struggling young Nobody, looking for my first big break.

The thing is, a famous food critic has to have a specialty. But there was only one thing that truly got my motor running: porridge.

So I scoured the world for the perfect bowl of porridge, but I could not find it. Until one day, deep in the woods, I came upon a small hut, with a neon sign flashing: PORRIDGE! HOT PORRIDGE!—The Three Bears Roadside Porridge Stand.

I went in. There was no one around. In no particular order I found: three chairs, three beds, and three bowls of porridge.

Model

Here are 6 bowls of porridge. What happens when you put them into 3 equal groups? Division!

6 divided into 3 equal groups = 2 bowls in each group

1. 8 divided into 2 equal groups = _______ bowls in each group

2. 12 divided into 4 equal groups = _______ bowls in each group

3. 15 divided into 3 equal groups = _______ bowls in each group

The rest of the story may sound familiar.

I sat. I slept. I ate. The chairs were: too small, too big, just right. Ditto the beds. But the bowls of porridge? Simply fantastic! My search was over. I had found the perfect porridge.

Then the bears arrived, asking: "Who's been sitting in my chair?" and so on. By then, I was already on my laptop, typing out my review. The headline: POSH PORRIDGE! 4 STARS! 3 BIG HOORAYS FOR THE 3 BEARS!

Snazzy, eh?

The rest, as they say, is history. Over night, I, Goldie Loxe Jones, went from "Who's That?" to "Goldie Loxe Jones, Famous Food Critic."

And I'm still famous today!

THE END

Fractured Fairy Tales Multiplication & Division • Scholastic Teaching Resources

Name ______________________________ Date ______________

Write a division problem for each picture. Find each quotient.

4. ____ ÷ 3 = ______ beds

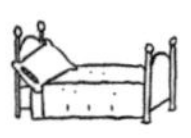
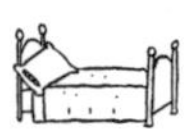

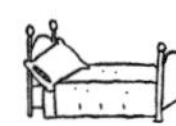

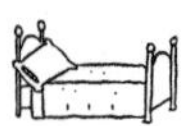

5. ______ ÷ ______ = ______ bowls

6. ______ ÷ ______ = ______ bears

Divide to find each quotient.

7. 16 ÷ 2 = ______ bowls

8. 20 ÷ 4 = ______ beds

9. 24 ÷ 6 = ______ bears

10. 36 ÷ 6 = ______ children

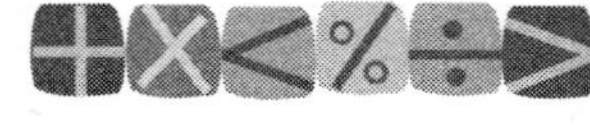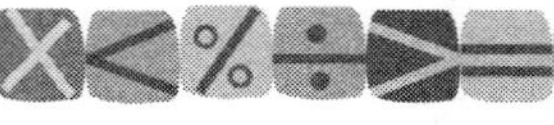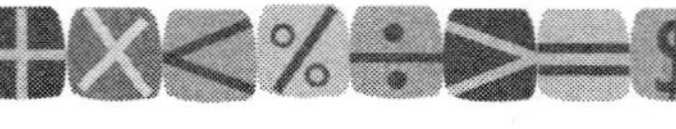

Concept of Division, Division Facts

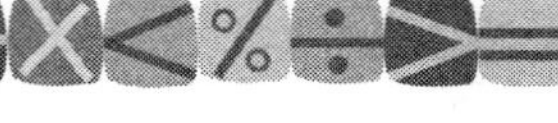

Name ______________________________ **Date** ____________________

Fill in the Division Facts table.

1 ÷ 1 =	2 ÷ 1 =	3 ÷ 1 =	4 ÷ 1 =	5 ÷ 1 =	6 ÷ 1 =	7 ÷ 1 =	8 ÷ 1 =	9 ÷ 1 =
2 ÷ 2 =	4 ÷ 2 =	6 ÷ 2 =	8 ÷ 2 =	10 ÷ 2 =	12 ÷ 2 =	14 ÷ 2 =	16 ÷ 2 =	18 ÷ 2 =
3 ÷ 3 =	6 ÷ 3 =	9 ÷ 3 =	12 ÷ 3 =	15 ÷ 3 =	18 ÷ 3 =	21 ÷ 3 =	24 ÷ 3 =	27 ÷ 3 =
4 ÷ 4 =	8 ÷ 4 =	12 ÷ 4 =	16 ÷ 4 =	20 ÷ 4 =	24 ÷ 4 =	28 ÷ 4 =	32 ÷ 4 =	36 ÷ 4 =
5 ÷ 5 =	10 ÷ 5 =	15 ÷ 5 =	20 ÷ 4 =	25 ÷ 5 =	30 ÷ 5 =	35 ÷ 5 =	40 ÷ 5 =	45 ÷ 5 =
6 ÷ 6 =	12 ÷ 6 =	18 ÷ 6 =	24 ÷ 6 =	30 ÷ 6 =	36 ÷ 6 =	42 ÷ 6 =	48 ÷ 6 =	54 ÷ 6 =
7 ÷ 7 =	14 ÷ 7 =	21 ÷ 7 =	28 ÷ 7 =	35 ÷ 7 =	42 ÷ 7 =	49 ÷ 7 =	56 ÷ 7 =	63 ÷ 7 =
8 ÷ 8 =	16 ÷ 8 =	24 ÷ 8 =	32 ÷ 8 =	40 ÷ 8 =	48 ÷ 8 =	56 ÷ 8 =	64 ÷ 8 =	72 ÷ 8 =
9 ÷ 9 =	18 ÷ 9 =	27 ÷ 9 =	36 ÷ 9 =	45 ÷ 9 =	54 ÷ 9 =	63 ÷ 9 =	72 ÷ 9 =	81 ÷ 9 =

Name ______________________________ Date ______________

The Lion and the Mouse

Once there was a small mouse who found herself deep in the forest caught in the paws of a mighty lion.

"I don't suppose you might consider letting me go, would you, big fella?" the mouse said.

The lion answered, "Not a chance." Then his eyes narrowed. "What's in it for me?" he asked.

"I'm likely to be rich and powerful some day," the mouse said. "And when that day comes, I'll help you out."

The lion had his doubts about this. A mouse—rich and powerful? Impossible! But he let the mouse go anyway.

"This may surprise you but, every once in a while, we lions like to do something nice," the lion said.

Time passed. The mouse did well in school, and ended up becoming a big-time lawyer.

Meanwhile, the lion became quite well known in Hollywood as a character actor. He played several different roles, including a tiger, a panther, and even a hyena (a part that got him an Oscar nomination).

But then the lion got involved in an ugly contract dispute with the studio. They wanted him to do a movie called *Mary Had a Little Lamb.* The lion wanted to do *Richard the Lion-Hearted.* The contract was iron-clad. There was no way out.

"I'm trapped!" cried the lion. "I'll never get out of this contract!"

Or so it seemed. Suddenly the mouse appeared in his office. "Remember me?" she said.

As the top contract lawyer in town, the mouse agreed to represent the lion in his case against the studio. A meeting was called between the two sides. The mouse opened the meeting by saying: "Sometimes, it's better to be a small mouse than a big lion."

"Is this one of those times?" asked the lion.

"No," said the mouse. "So I'd like to introduce you all to a very special friend of mine. Mr. Bear, you can come in now."

And with that, the mouse opened a door and in came a ferocious bear who roared so loud that the studio lawyers immediately ran away in terror.

"We give in!" they cried, flinging their papers as they ran. "We'll do anything you say!"

"Well," said the mouse, after the studio lawyers were gone, "Looks like we won that case."

"How can I ever thank you, small mouse?" said the lion.

"You already thanked me," said the mouse.

"By letting you go years ago when we were on the trail?" the lion said.

"No," said the mouse. "Your secretary wrote me a check for my legal services."

"Oh," said the lion.

And the moral of the story is: It's good to be right, but it's even better to have a good lawyer.

THE END

Multiplication Problems and Facts

Name ______________________ **Date** ____________

Model

Suppose the lion does about 7 good deeds a year. In 4 years, how many total good deeds would the lion do?

Answer: 28 good deeds

2005	2006	2007	2008
☺☺☺☺☺☺☺	☺☺☺☺☺☺☺	☺☺☺☺☺☺☺	☺☺☺☺☺☺☺

7 x 4 = 28

____

1. The mouse became the boss of a large law firm with 8 lawyers. Each lawyer had 3 clients at a time. How many clients were there in all?

____

2. The lion's greatest movie role was playing a hyena in *The Lonely Hyena*. To learn a hyena accent, the lion needed to practice 6 hours a day for 9 days. How many hours did he practice?

____

3. The mouse pays the bear 8 dollars per roar. How much money would the bear make for 4 roars?

____

4. The new movie *The Mouse and the Lion* tells the story of the mouse and the lion. The advertising budget call for 8 ads on TV for 9 nights in a row. How many ads will this be?

____

5. *The Mouse and the Lion* earned 8 million dollars per week for its first 3 weeks. Then it earned 6 million for the next 4 weeks. How much did it make in all?

____

6. A family of 5 went to see *The Mouse and the Lion.* If each ticket cost $7 and each person bought a popcorn that cost $3, how much did the family spend altogether?

____

7. **(Challenge)** How much would the family in problem 6 save if they went to the early bird matinee where tickets are only $5 and popcorn is reduced to $2?

____

8. **(Challenge)** Which would be more— roaring 7 times for 8 dollars per roar, or 6 roars for 9 dollars per roar? How much more?

____

Name ______________________ Date ______________

Turtle Gets a Makeover

Turtle had never been a fast runner, so when Raccoon bragged that he could improve her speed, Turtle was all ears.

"Could you really do that?" Turtle asked.

"You're only as fast as you think you are," Raccoon said.

"I've always thought of myself as slow," Turtle said.

"Then it's time to change your thinking," Raccoon said.

Racoon had Turtle do all sorts of speed drills.

"Do you think these drills will make me faster?" Turtle asked.

"Speed is a state of mind," Raccoon said.

Model

Turtle ran 12 yards in 3 minutes. At this rate, how many yards did she run each minute?

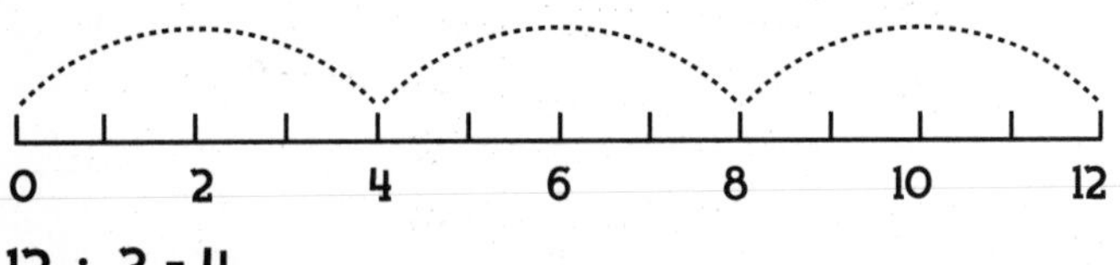

12 ÷ 3 = 4

Answer: 4 yards

1. "Try again," Raccoon said. So Turtle tried again and ran 16 yards in 4 minutes. How many yards per minute did she run now?

   ____

2. "You want to see some real speed?" Raccoon said. "Watch this." So Raccoon ran 27 feet without stopping. If a yard is 3 feet, how many yards did Raccoon run?

   ____

3. Next, Raccoon ran 48 feet at a speed of 6 feet per second. "Now that's speedy," Raccoon said. How many seconds did it take to run this distance?

   ____

Raccoon put Turtle on a special exercise program. She did push-ups, sit-ups, knee-bends, and roll-overs.

4. Every day, Turtle did the same number of push-ups for 6 days. In all, she did 42 push-ups. How many did she do each day?

   ____

5. Every day, Turtle did the same number of sit-ups for 1 week. In all, she did 63 sit-ups. How many did she do each day?

   ____

Raccoon then gave Turtle a complete makeover. He polished Turtle's shell until it was shiny. He painted racing stripes to make the shell look speedy and streamlined.

"Do you feel fast now?" Raccoon asked Turtle.

"I really do," Turtle said.

"Good," Raccoon said. "Because you're only as fast as you think you are." At this point, Rabbit showed up.

"What's with Turtle?" Rabbit asked.

"I gave her a complete makeover," Raccoon said. "She's now lightning fast. She can beat you in a race."

Division Problems and Facts

Name ______________________ **Date** ______________

"Is that true?" Rabbit said. "We'll see."

So a race was set.

At the starting line Rabbit and Turtle eyed one another. Rabbit wore nothing special, but Turtle wore spiked running shoes, a running hat, and running goggles that made her look, well, ridiculous.

Rabbit could not stop laughing. The starting gun went off. Turtle leaped into the lead.

Rabbit laughed.

Turtle barreled on ahead. Rabbit still laughed. Was Turtle faster than usual? Rabbit couldn't tell, because he was too busy laughing.

Rabbit kept laughing until Turtle had almost reached the finish line. Then he dashed off in an attempt to catch up. Just before he was about to pass Turtle, Rabbit once more fell into a laughing fit.

He rolled over sideways as Turtle crossed the finish line.

"The winner and new champ," Raccoon cried, "TURTLE!"

Which just goes to show: You're only as fast as you think you are—or something like that.

6. During the first part of the race, Turtle ran 24 yards at a speed of 4 yards per minute. How long did it take to run this distance?

____

7. During the next part of the race, Turtle ran another 20 yards in 4 minutes. How many yards did she run per minute?

____

8. As the race was ending Rabbit ran 72 yards at a speed of 9 yards per second. How long did it take to run this distance?

____

9. **(Challenge)** Turtle received a $24 prize for her victory. List the different ways can she divide her prize into equal-sized amounts.

____

THE END

Name ______________________ Date ____________

How to Break Out of the Dungeon

Does this sound like you: You're tired all the time? You spend your days in a dark hole? You eat bread and water for dinner every night? If so, then you need my new book . . .

Yes, more and more citizens of our fair kingdom are finding themselves locked in the Royal Dungeon for many, many years—and think there's not a thing they can do about it. Until now!

Don't believe it? I'm Hobart the Lesser. I got out of the dungeon—and so can you. Just follow the easy steps in my new book. Take a look at what these satisfied customers had to say.

Name: Duff the Stout
Crime: Stole a crust of bread
Sentence: 60 years
I thought I was done for. Then I got your book. I never realized I could get out of this dungeon by escaping through a tunnel. Now, all I need to do is dig that tunnel—and I'm OUTTA HERE! Thanks a lot, Hobart the Lesser!

Name: Yana
Crime: Coughed during a music performance of the king's son
Sentence: 75 years
Your book is amazing. In Chapter 3, I learned that if a handsome prince came to kiss me, I might turn into a frog and be able to hop through the bars of my cell. Thanks, Hobart the Lesser!

Name: Gomm the Tedious
Crime: Told dull jokes during lunch with the king
Sentence: 200 years
I used to feel that my life was going nowhere in this dungeon. But now, thanks to Hobart the Lesser, I'm studying to be a powerful sorcerer. Before long, I'll be able to cast spells so powerful, I'll just WALK out of this dungeon. Thanks, Hobart, you're the best!

Heard enough? Now you, too, can end your "dungeon habit." So don't wait another day for your dungeon sentence to pass. Get Hobart the Lesser's fabulous new book *How to Break Out of the Dungeon*. And if you act today, we'll send you, absolutely free, Hobart's companion book, *How to Avoid Being Thrown in the Dungeon in the First Place*. You'll love it!

THE END

Mixed (Multistep) Division and Multiplication Fact Problems

Name ______________________ Date ____________

Model

Duff the Stout has spent 49 days in the dungeon. How many 7-day weeks is this?

49 ÷ 7 = 7

Answer: 7 weeks

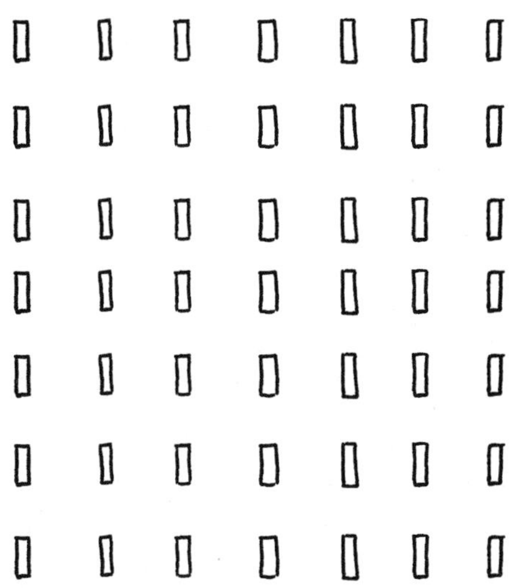

1. The guards give each prisoner 6 ounces of thin soup per day. In 8 days, how many ounces would each prisoner get?

   ____

2. Chapter 4 of Hobart's book is called "Bribe Your Way Out of the Dungeon." If Yana gives the guard bribes of 6 ducats per month for 9 months, what will her total bribe be?

   ____

3. For his first sorcery lessons, Gomm paid 4 ducats a week for 6 weeks. Then for his advanced lessons, he paid 5 ducats a week for the next 7 weeks. How much did he pay in all?

   ____

4. The Tunnel-Co Tunnel Company advertised its Basic Tunnel for 100 ducats. Duff has 40 ducats. If he saves 6 ducats a month, how many more months will it take to have enough for a tunnel?

   ____

5. Suppose Duff is able to save only 5 ducats per month instead of 6 in problem 4. How many months will it take to get the tunnel?

   ____

6. The guards have 100 ounces of thin soup for the weekend. How many bowls of soup can be served if the bowls each hold 4 ounces?

   ____

7. The night guard receives bribes of 3 ducats a month from 3 different prisoners. How much will the guard receive from these 3 prisoners over 9 months?

   ____

8. Hobart's book has 9 chapters and 120 pages. Chapter 1 is 48 pages long. The rest of the chapters all have the same number of pages. How many pages does each of these chapters have?

   ____

9. Mogg's sentence of 75 days was reduced by 41 days for "good behavior." Then 22 days were added to her sentence for "no reason at all." How many weeks must Mogg serve?

   ____

Name ______________________________ Date ______________

I Married a Beast!

First off I want to explain. My name is Betty. Though I'm not bad-looking, no one has ever called me "Beauty" before, not even as a nickname.

But I did marry a beast.

Here's how it happened. When a young Beast named Walter proposed to me, at first I thought, "*No way*!" But when I reread the original Beauty and the Beast story, it suddenly dawned on me: *He's going to turn into a handsome young prince before I know it.*

So, to everyone's surprise, I told Walter, the beast, "*Yes, I'll marry you.*"

At the most, I figured I'd need to suffer through a few weeks of beastliness.

Not a chance. As the weeks passed, Walter still didn't change. I kept computing the days. After a while, I worked out a method to compute the days from weeks using mental math.

Model

7 x 10 weeks
Multiply 7 x 1, then attach 1 zero → 70

7 x 20 weeks
Multiply 7 x 2, then attach 1 zero → 140

Use mental math to solve these problems.

1. 7 x 30 = _______

2. 7 x 40 = _______

3. 4 x 10 = _______

4. 6 x 10 = _______

5. 4 x 20 = _______

6. 6 x 20 = _______

7. 4 x 30 = _______

8. 6 x 40 = _______

9. 4 x 50 = _______

10. 6 x 80 = _______

Keep in mind, we got married more than four years ago.

Of course, the whole time, my mother kept telling me, "He's a *beast*!"

As if I didn't know. But I insisted things would get better. As beasts go, Walter was a great guy, with a good heart. So it was only a matter of time until he "went handsome," as they say.

Well, time passed. All my friends were very understanding. "He may be a beast now," they said, "but you just wait."

So I waited.

If anything, Walter was worse. He was getting more beastly. One day I said to him, "Have you looked in a mirror lately, Walter?"

"Hey," he said, "I don't like being a beast any more than you do!"

We went to a doctor. A beast specialist. Who examined him every which way.

Mental Math Multiplication

Name ______________________________ Date ______________

Model

How much would it cost to visit a specialist who charged $100 a visit for 8 visits?

8 x 100
Multiply 8 x 1, then attach 2 zeroes → $800

Use mental math to solve these problems.

11. 8 x 200
Multiply 8 x 2, attach 2 zeroes → ________

12. 8 x 500
Multiply 8 x 5, attach 2 zeroes → ________

13. 5 x 100 = ________

14. 7 x 100 = ________

15. 5 x 300 = ________

16. 7 x 200 = ________

17. 4 x 500 = ________

"Your husband is a beast," the specialist told me. Tell me something I don't know.

Basically it ends up like this. He might turn into a handsome prince tomorrow. Or next year. Or ten years from now. Then again, he might not. The beast doctor wasn't sure.

But here's the good part. You get used to it. And no one ever ignores us. Not in stores or restaurants or anywhere else.

"Yes sir!" they say. "Yes sir, Mister Beast."

So when all is said and done, I guess being married to a beast is not that bad. Who ever guessed I would end up saying that?

THE END

Model

As months turned into weeks, I devised new ways to count the days using mental math.

30 x 20
Multiply 3 x 2, attach 2 zeroes → 600

300 x 20
Multiply 3 x 2, attach 3 zeroes → 6,000

300 x 200
Multiply 3 x 2, attach 4 zeroes → 60,000

---

18. 400 x 20 = ________

19. 400 x 200 = ________

20. 500 x 40 = ________

21. 500 x 600 = ________

22. **(Challenge)** Use mental math to find the product of 3,000 x 500. How many zeroes did you attach?

____

Name ______________________ Date ____________

Interview With a Fool

Hello, and welcome to The Big Interview *on Channel F, the Fairy Tale Channel. I'm Pillow Jones, your host. Tonight on F, an interview with Bascomb the Fool,our kingdom's Top Fool and Official Royal Numbskull.*

Pillow: Hello and welcome to the show, Mr. Fool.

Fool: Thank you, it's a privilege to be here.

Pillow: You've been the Royal Fool for 14 years now. How have things changed during your time?

Fool: When I first started, the focus was more on being a complete knucklehead. Now the trend is moving more toward being an absolute nitwit.

Pillow: Are you an absolute nitwit?

Fool: Does a chicken have lips?

Pillow: Hmm, I'm not sure. Tell us about your childhood. Did you always want to be a fool?

Fool: Growing up I was more of a nincompoop. But then, in college, I began to focus on doing really stupid things.

Pillow: Such as?

Fool: Well, I put gum in my hair, on purpose!

Pillow: Anything else?

Fool: I often put my socks on over my shoes.

Pillow: Fascinating. How did you get your first big break?

Fool: When the previous fool got thrown in the dungeon, I took over.

Pillow: Describe the perfect day for Bascomb the Fool.

Fool: I get up. I get through the day without being thrown in the dungeon. Then I go to sleep.

Pillow: You seem preoccupied with being thrown in the dungeon. Why is that?

Fool: Because it's dark, cold, full of rats, and they might chain you to the wall.

Pillow: You're a successful fool. Surely the king wouldn't throw you in the dungeon!

Fool: Of course he would. In a heartbeat.

Pillow: What do you do on your days off?

Fool: Sometimes I'm so tired of doing stupid things that I'll do something smart—just for a change of pace. I'll read a difficult book or solve mental math problems.

Pillow: And other times?

Fool: I'll just sit and stare at my toes.

Pillow: Where does Bascomb the Fool hope to be a year from now?

Fool: Not in the dungeon.

Pillow: How about five or ten years from now?

Fool: Still not in the dungeon.

Pillow: That's your only ambition? Not to be in the dungeon?

Fool: Yes.

Pillow: Anything else you'd like to say to our millions of viewers before we say good night?

Fool: Yes, if you think *I'm* a fool, try looking in the mirror, pal.

Pillow: Good night, Mr. Fool.

Fool: Good night yourself, Pillow.

THE END

Mental Math Division

Name ______________________________ Date ______________

Model

One day, the King said to me, "Fool, what is 150 divided by 3?" Well I didn't have a pencil and paper. But I devised a way to do division MENTALLY.

150 ÷ 3
Divide 15 ÷ 3, then attach a zero → 50

120 ÷ 2
Divide 12 ÷ 2, then attach a zero → 60

Model

Dividing larger numbers just means attaching more zeroes.

1800 ÷ 3
Divide 18 ÷ 3, attach two zeroes → 600

1500 ÷ 5
Divide 15 ÷ 5, attach two zeroes → 300

Use mental math to solve these problems.

1. 180 ÷ 3 = _______
2. 350 ÷ 5 = _______
3. 90 ÷ 3 = _______
4. 210 ÷ 3 = _______
5. 240 ÷ 4 = _______
6. 320 ÷ 8 = _______
7. 360 ÷ 6 = _______
8. 490 ÷ 7 = _______
9. 640 ÷ 8 = _______
10. 360 ÷ 9 = _______
11. 2400 ÷ 4 = ______
12. 2500 ÷ 5= ______
13. 1400 ÷ 2 = ______
14. 2400 ÷ 3 = ______
15. 2800 ÷ 7 = ______
16. 7200 ÷ 8 = ______
17. 6300 ÷ 7 = ______
18. 3600 ÷ 6 = ______
19. 20,000 ÷ 2 = ______
20. **(Challenge)** 180 ÷ 30 = ______
What happens when you have a zero in the divisor?

____

____

Name ______________________________ Date ______________

Advice From Morris the Wise One

Morris the Wise One is a licensed Royal Wise Man and practicing Sagacious Fellow. He has a Master's Degree in Deep Thought from Medieval University. He has been advising the King for many years, and has (almost) never been thrown in the dungeon.

Dear Wise One,

Recently, I was about to leap when someone yelled "Look!" Does it really help to look before you leap?

Signed, Leland the Leaper

Dear Lee,

It depends on where you're looking and leaping. Let's say you're about to leap over a 87-foot high castle wall with 4 hungry crocodiles below. Then it probably pays to look. On the other hand, for a lower wall with fewer crocodiles (or crocodiles that are not hungry) you might be better off just to leap. My rule of thumb is: Multiply the height of the leap by the number of hungry crocodiles. If the number is over 300, you should probably look before you leap.

Sincerely, Morris the Wise One

Model

You can ESTIMATE before you look or leap. First round any "hard" numbers. Then use mental math. Hint: Round to the nearest 10.

87-foot wall x 4 hungry crocs → 90 x 4 = 360 (Look!)
53-foot wall x 5 hungry crocs → 50 x 5 = 250 (Leap!)

---

1. 37-foot wall x 9 hungry crocs →
   40 x 9 = _______

2. 69-foot wall x 6 hungry crocs →
   _______ x 6 = _______

Use estimation to solve these problems.

3. 34 x 4 = _______

4. 63 x 2 = _______

5. 47 x 5 = _______

6. 28 x 4 = _______

7. 58 x 3 = _______

8. 67 x 7 = _______

Estimating: Multiplication

Name ______________________ Date ____________

Dear Wise One,

Recently, I was told that a stitch in time saves nine. Is this true? If not, then how many stitches does it actually save?

Signed, Interested in the Answer

Dear Interested,

Current research shows that each stitch in time can save a lot more than 9. For example, Brad Finster of Finster, Ohio, saved 23 stitches for those he made in time.

Sincerely, Morris the Wise One

Model

You can ESTIMATE the number of stitches you save. Round each number. Then use mental math to multiply.

23 stitches made x 11 stitches saved →
20 x 10 = 200

9. 41 stitches made x 13 stitches saved →
   40 x 10 = _______

10. 57 stitches made x 21 stitches saved →
    60 x 20 = _______

11. 77 stitches made x 42 stitches saved →
    80 x _______ = _______

12. 91 stitches made x 56 stitches saved →
    _______ x _______ = _______

Estimate the products.

13. 31 x 13 = _______

14. 33 x 19 = _______

15. 48 x 51 = _______

16. 71 x 49 = _______

Dear Wise One,

Is it true that watched pots never boil and you should never judge a book by its cover?

Signed, Book Worm Pot-Watcher

Dear Worm,

Somewhat true. What is absolutely true is that watched books never boil and that you can never judge a pot by its cover.

Sincerely, Morris the Wise One

17. Morris's new book, *Wise Cracks*, has 21 chapters. Each chapter has 28 pages. Estimate the number of pages in the book.

    ____

18. Morris's book sells for $29. Estimate how much 58 books cost.

    ____

THE END

Name ______________________ Date ____________

More Advice From Morris the Wise One

Morris the Wise One is a licensed Royal Wise Man and practicing Sagacious Fellow. He has a Master's Degree in Deep Thought from Medieval University. He has been advising the King for many years, and has (almost) never been thrown in the dungeon.

Dear Wise One,

Recently I was told that the early bird catches the worm. If this is true, what does the late bird catch?

Signed, Nightcrawler

Dear Night,

The late bird catches a lot of things. For example, last week the late bird caught 92 worms in 3 days. Now I ask you, on the average, how many worms did the late bird catch each day?

Sincerely, Morris the Wise One

Model

Use estimation to divide. First round the "hard" numbers to make them easy to divide. Then use mental math.

92 worms ÷ 3 days → 90 ÷ 3 = 3 worms

1. 149 ÷ 5 → 150 ÷ 5 = _______
2. 213 ÷ 7 → 210 ÷ 7 = _______
3. 418 ÷ 6 → 420 ÷ 6 = _______
4. 322 ÷ 8 → _______ ÷ 8 = _______

Use estimation to solve these problems.

5. 76 ÷ 4 = _______
6. 59 ÷ 6 = _______
7. 162 ÷ 2 = _______
8. 273 ÷ 3 = _______
9. 555 ÷ 7 = _______
10. 479 ÷ 6 = _______
11. 632 ÷ 9 = _______
12. 717 ÷ 8 = _______

Estimating: Division

Name ______________________________ Date ______________

Dear Wise One,

Recently, I was told that good things come in small packages. Is this true?

Signed, Confused

Dear Confused,

It depends. Suppose a $137 necklace came in a 3-ounce package. How much do you think this package would be worth per ounce?

Sincerely, Morris the Wise One

Model

Sometimes you need to round to a number that is easy to divide. Instead of rounding 137 to 140, round to 150 because 150 is easy to divide by 3.

137 ÷ 3 → 140 ÷ 3 → 150 ÷ 3 = 50

13. 238 ÷ 5 → 240 ÷ 5 → _______ ÷ 5 = _______

14. 372 ÷ 6 → _______ ÷ _______ = _______

Round to an easy number, then estimate the quotient.

15. 109 ÷ 4 = _______

16. 311 ÷ 4 = _______

17. 266 ÷ 7 = _______

18. 433 ÷ 6 = _______

Dear Wise One,

Recently, I got a bird in the hand. But then I saw two in the bush. Which is better?

Signed, Bird Man

Dear Man,

The birds in the bush. Recently, I counted not 2 birds in 1 bush, but 413 birds in 22 bushes! Clearly, this is better than a bird in the hand. By the way, can you calculate the average number of birds in the 22 bushes?

Sincerely, Morris the Wise One

Model

Sometimes you need to round both dividend and divisor to get easier numbers.

413 ÷ 22 → 410 ÷ 20 → 400 ÷ 20 = 20

242 ÷ 47 → 240 ÷ 50 → 250 ÷ 50 = 5

Round to an easy number, then estimate the quotient.

19. 438 ÷ 87 → 440 ÷ 90 → _______ ÷ 90 = _______

20. 107 ÷ 54 = _______

21. 151 ÷ 29 = _______

22. 627 ÷ 72 = _______

THE END

Name ______________________ Date ____________

The Prime Minister's Dog

Long ago, in a very up-and-coming kingdom, there was an up-and-coming young government minister named Carp. Minister Carp was very handsome and charming. But was he smart?

Not really.

It didn't matter though, because Minister Carp had a really smart dog. This dog did everything for the minister. The dog wrote his speeches and made his decisions. The dog submitted laws and proposals. At every step of the way, the dog told the minister what to do.

In time, Minister Carp became *Prime Minister* Carp. On the eve of his election, Carp gave a brilliant—speech (written by the dog). After the speech—which everyone loved—the minister called the dog into his office.

"You're fired," the Prime Minister said.

Fired? The dog was stunned. What now?

Model

There were 3 villages in District A. Each village had 14 votes. How many votes were there in all?

14	→	^{1}14	→	^{1}14
x3		x3		x3
		2		42

Find each product.

1. 28 x2

2. 36 x3

3. 43 x4

4. 35 x3

5. 53 x7

6. 72 x5

7. 47 x6

8. 46 x7

9. 78 x8

10. 89 x5

As time passed, the dashing Prime Minister Carp became ever more popular in the kingdom. The dog became ever more jealous. *Why should he profit from my ideas?* thought the dog.

So, the dog made a decision. It would run for Prime Minister. A debate was scheduled shortly before the election.

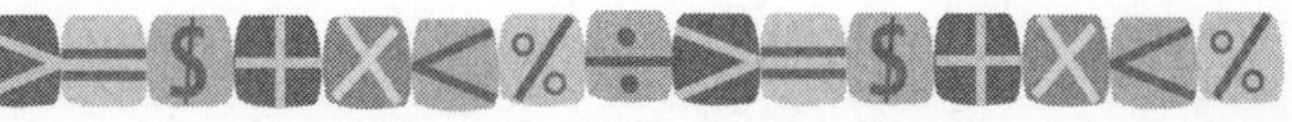

Name ______________________________ **Date** ______________

At the debate, the Prime Minister spoke first. To tell the truth, he said nothing new or interesting. But he was very handsome and made a splendid impression on the audience.

Next the dog got up to speak. The dog's speech was brilliant. It was daring and imaginative. But who heard it? When the dog got up to speak the audience started to hoot.

"A dog!" they laughed. "Sit down, pooch!"

"Bow wow!" others jeered.

The dog tried to speak, but they kept jeering.

Finally the dog left the stage. In a few days, the dog quit the campaign and retired from politics. Today, the dog lives on a farm and does the things most dogs do—takes walks, fetches bones, naps, and so on.

The moral of the story? Don't expect the world to be fair—especially if you're a dog.

THE END

Model

The audience was divided into four sections with 374 people in each section. How many people were there in all?

384	→	$3^{1}84$	→	$^{2}3^{1}84$	→	$^{2}3^{1}84$
x 4		x 3		x 3		x 3
		2		52		1152

11. 733 x 4

12. 483 x 5

13. 626 x 6

14. 584 x 7

15. 895 x 6

16. 397 x 9

17. The dog served Minister Carp for 6 years. How many days was this?
(Hint: There are 365 days in one year.)

____

18. Minister Carp bought 7 suits. Each suit cost 408 ducats. In all, how many ducats did Carp spend?

____

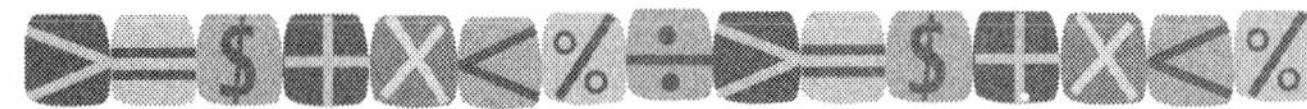

Name ______________________________ Date ______________

Medieval Monarch Magazine

For the Ruler Who Has Everything (and Wants More!)

Table of Contents

Fractured Fairy Tales Multiplication & Division • Scholastic Teaching Resources

2-Digit Multiplication

Name ______________________ Date ____________

Model

A single royal feaster consumes 46 morsels of food per feast. How many morsels will 43 feasters consume?

$$\begin{array}{r} 46 \\ \times\ 43 \\ \hline \end{array} \rightarrow \begin{array}{r} {}^{1}46 \\ \times\ 43 \\ \hline 138 \end{array} \rightarrow \begin{array}{r} {}^{2}{}^{1}46 \\ \times\ 43 \\ \hline 138 \\ 1840 \end{array} \rightarrow \begin{array}{r} {}^{2}{}^{1}46 \\ \times\ 43 \\ \hline 138 \\ 1840 \\ \hline 1978 \end{array}$$

1. 46 x 24

2. 63 x 25

3. 73 x 38

4. 79 x 42

5. 78 x 15

6. 35 x 13

7. 42 x 36

8. 73 x 24

9. 36 x 33

10. 86 x 24

11. The Royal Tax Collector collected 58 ducats from 31 different farmers. How many ducats were collected in all?

____

12. Rolvar the Scribe got a product of 5036 when he multiplied 48 by 82. Estimate: Does Rolvar's answer sound correct to you? Explain.

____

____

____

Name ____________________ Date __________

The Snake in the River

A young prince was walking along the river when he happened to see a snake on a log.

"Help me!" the snake said. "I fell asleep basking on this log. Now the log has floated to the middle of the river. I'm stuck! I can't swim."

"Why should I help a snake?" asked the prince. "What can you do for me?"

"You can tell me your troubles," the snake said. "I am clever at helping people with their problems."

"Hmm," thought the prince. He *did* have some troubles. A beautiful princess had recently rejected him. And this was after hours of telling her how strong, handsome, and wonderful he was.

"Your problem is that you're too self-centered," said the snake. "Go and see the young lady again. Instead of talking only about yourself, talk about *her*."

"Hmm," said the prince. "That sounds like a good idea. If it works I will return and free you from your log."

The prince followed the snake's advice—and it worked. The princess was delighted, and soon she invited the prince for a ride along the river. Before long, they came to the very place where the snake was stuck on the log.

Model

The snake drifted 78 feet in 3 hours at a steady rate. How many feet did the snake drift each hour? Use division to find the quotient.

$3\overline{)78} \rightarrow \begin{array}{r} 2 \\ 3\overline{)78} \\ -6 \\ \hline 1 \end{array} \rightarrow \begin{array}{r} 2 \\ 3\overline{)78} \\ -6\downarrow \\ \hline 18 \end{array} \rightarrow \begin{array}{r} 26 \\ 3\overline{)78} \\ -6 \\ \hline 18 \\ -18 \\ \hline 0 \end{array}$

Find each quotient.

1. $3\overline{)39}$
2. $4\overline{)48}$
3. $6\overline{)66}$
4. $5\overline{)95}$
5. $3\overline{)93}$
6. $2\overline{)78}$
7. $6\overline{)96}$
8. $7\overline{)98}$

1-Digit Long Division

Name ______________________________ Date ______________

"Over here! Prince!" the snake cried.

"Who's that?" asked the princess.

"Oh, it's just a snake," the prince said. "He helped me before and now he wants me to help him. But I won't do it."

"Why not?" asked the princess.

"Snakes are low creatures," said the prince. "You can't trust them.

"Well, I think you should help the snake," said the princess. "After all, the snake helped you. It's only fair."

With that, the prince waded out in the water, picked up the snake, and was promptly bitten on the arm.

"Yow!" the prince howled at the painful, yet nonpoisonous, wound.

"What did you do that for?" the princess asked.

"Creatures behave the way you expect them to behave," said the snake. "The prince expected treachery. So treachery was what he got."

THE END

Model

Before they met up with the snake, the prince and princess rode 152 feet in 8 seconds at a steady pace. How many feet did they ride each second?

$$8\overline{)152} \rightarrow \begin{array}{r} 1 \\ 8\overline{)152} \\ -8 \\ \hline 7 \end{array} \rightarrow \begin{array}{r} 1 \\ 8\overline{)152} \\ -8\downarrow \\ \hline 72 \end{array} \rightarrow \begin{array}{r} 19 \\ 8\overline{)152} \\ -8 \\ \hline 72 \\ -72 \\ \hline 0 \end{array}$$

Find each quotient.

9. $2\overline{)146}$

10. $4\overline{)168}$

11. $5\overline{)185}$

12. $6\overline{)198}$

13. $7\overline{)168}$

14. $5\overline{)225}$

15. $8\overline{)456}$

16. $9\overline{)324}$

Name ______________________________ Date ______________

Channel F Presents: Happily Ever After

Hello, and welcome to Happily Ever After on Channel F, the Fairy Tale Channel. I'm Pillow Jones, your host. Tonight, live via Talking Mirror satellite technology, we bring you Princess Brier Rose, a.k.a. Sleeping Beauty.

Pillow: Hello, Rose. This is Pillow Jones from Happily Ever After. Can you hear me all right through your Talking Mirror satellite hook-up?

Rose: (*yawning*) Yes, fine Pillow. I'm a little tired, that's all. I just woke up.

Pillow: So, Rose tell us about what's been going on since we last saw you?

Rose: Well, as you may know, I ran into a string of bad luck. First, an evil witch cast a spell on me. Then I pricked my finger on a poison spindle. Then, I slept for 100 years. Finally, things worked out when I was kissed by a handsome prince.

Pillow: How did things go from there?

Rose: Well, we were supposed to live happily ever after. But there was one problem. We had no castle. We had to move in with the King and Queen.

Pillow: Living with your in-laws? Ugh!

Rose: Tell me about it! I told the prince it was them or me. So we finally moved out—on the morning of my 126th birthday!

Pillow: Wait a second. You're a *126 years old*?

Rose: Well of course! If you sleep for 100 years, you tend to age rather quickly, you know. In any event, my husband swears I don't look a day over 120—Ha ha!

Model

How many months is 126 years? Multiply 126 by 12.

126	→	1[1]26	→	1[1]26	→	1[1]26
x 12		x 12		x 12		x 12
		252		252		252
				1260		1260
						1512

1. 472 x 21

2. 213 x 43

3. 305 x 16

4. 281 x 42

5. 643 x 35

6. 734 x 19

7. 694 x 47

8. 883 x 77

Fractured Fairy Tales Multiplication & Division • Scholastic Teaching Resources

3-Digit Multiplication

Name ______________________________ Date ______________

Rose: Just last week, we finally bought our own castle. Guess what? The place is a mess! The roof leaks, the drawbridge is rusty, and the moat needs dredging, and so on. The place is going to need a major face-lift!

Pillow: That's a lot of gelt, Rose, if you don't mind my saying so! So where will you get the money?

Rose: At first we thought we'd work for it! But then, honestly, Pillow. What can we do? He's a prince. I'm a princess. We don't *work*! So, we decided to raise the money the old-fashioned way—

Pillow: Wait, don't tell me. You raised taxes on the peasants. Brilliant!

Rose: It is brilliant, isn't it? Anyway, here's the plan. Each peasant pays us 376 ducats per month for the 482 months. Or its equivalent in cows, pumpkin seeds, bushels of oats, or in some cases, weasel pelts.

Pillow: That sounds like an excellent plan. When are you moving in?

Rose: Well, I'm not sure. And if you don't mind, I think I've had enough of this interview, Pillow. I'm feeling kind of sleepy.

Pillow: So there you have it, folks. This is Pillow Jones reporting live from the land of Sleeping Beauty. Good night, and remember, Live Happily Ever After!

Rose: (*yawning*) G'night.

THE END

Model

To find out how much the peasants have to pay, multiply 482 by 376.

	→		→		→	
482		$^{4}4^{1}82$		$^{5}4^{1}82$		$^{2}4^{1}82$
x 376		x 376		x 376		x 376
		2892		2892		2892
				33740		33740
						144600
						181232

9. 365
   x 594

10. 455
   x 586

11. 645
   x 481

12. 656
   x 126

13. 483
   x 578

14. 596
   x 588

15. 782
   x 996

16. 898
   x 769

Name ______________________ Date __________

The Two Warthogs

Two warthogs lived in the same hole. One warthog was beautiful—at least as warthogs go. The other was ugly—again, at least as warthogs go.

The beautiful warthog was always getting visitors. Warthog boyfriends crowded around. They brought flowers and gifts—the kind of rotting food that warthogs love to eat. They acted as if the ugly warthog didn't exist.

"Why should *she* get all the attention, and I get none?" the ugly warthog asked herself.

By and by it became known that a Hollywood studio was about to make a movie that included a key part for a warthog. A producer was coming to hold auditions for the part.

Hollywood!

There was much talk of the auditions in the warthog village. Of course, everyone agreed that the beautiful warthog would be perfect for the part.

The day came for the auditions. One by one the warthogs appeared and said their lines.

"Thank you very much," the producer said to each contestant.

Model

The producer scheduled 180 minutes for 7 auditions. How long should each audition last? How much time will be left over?

```
    25 R5
7 | 180
   -14
     40
    -35
      5
```

The remainder of 5 shows that there will be 5 minutes left over after the last audition.

Hint: The remainder must always be SMALLER than the divisor.

Write each quotient with a remainder.

1. 4 ⟌102

2. 3 ⟌88

3. 8 ⟌147

4. 6 ⟌197

5. 3 ⟌854

6. 4 ⟌458

Name ______________________________ Date ______________

7. $8\overline{)747}$

8. $6\overline{)295}$

9. $7\overline{)806}$

10. $6\overline{)567}$

Finally, it was the beautiful warthog's turn. She said her lines flawlessly.

"Thank you very much," said the producer.

Then a surprise. The ugly warthog stood to read her lines.

What's she doing here? thought the beautiful warthog.

The ugly warthog also read her lines well. When she was finished, the producer smiled and said, "I think we've got a winner!"

The ugly warthog was whisked away to Hollywood, where she appeared in the movie. She then went on to enjoy a successful career for many years playing warthogs in a variety of movies.

One day, many years later, the beautiful warthog visited Hollywood and came to the ugly warthog's dressing room. After catching up on old times, the beautiful warthog could not help but ask:

"What went wrong? I was beautiful. Everyone liked me. And no one liked you. Yet you ended up being a movie star. And me? A nobody. Why you rather than me?"

"That's simple," said the ugly warthog. "Beauty isn't everything. Not for a warthog, anyway. Here, they want a warthog to be a warthog. It's that simple. And that's why I'm a success."

The beautiful warthog could not argue with this logic. So she went home and never worried about Hollywood again.

THE END

11. The beautiful warthog started her own Beautiful Warthog Beauty Shop. She scheduled 95 minutes for 4 customers. How many minutes were scheduled for each customer? How many minutes were left over?

____

12. The Beautiful Warthog Beauty Shop had 113 customers in its first 4 weeks. How many customers did it have on the average each week?

____

Name ______________________________ Date ______________

Johnny Icarus and Ed Dedalus

Johnny Icarus wasn't much. He wasn't that good-looking. He couldn't sing all that well, and he couldn't dance. But boy, could that Johnny Icarus play the guitar!

Dee-ow, dee-ow, deee-aaah, dee-ow dee-ow dee-ow!

The audience screamed, "GO, JOHNNY, GO!"

The thing is, Johnny Icarus didn't actually have a guitar. He didn't *need* a guitar. He did it all with his mouth, making it sound just like real guitar: *Dee-ow, dee-dee-do-w-w-w!*

It wasn't long before he was signed by Dedalus Records. Ed Dedalus himself signed Johnny. A hit album followed: *Johnny-A-Go-Go!*

Critics raved. Audiences bought millions. Soon, Johnny Icarus was a star and he opened a glitzy stage show in Las Vegas.

But the Johnny Icarus Show wasn't just any show. It was the most spectacular show in town, folks said.

That is, except for Sunny Biggs. Sunny was the undisputed King of Las Vegas. The "Sun Man" was known far and wide. Nobody's show was as big as Sunny's—*nobody's*.

Until Johnny came along.

"A word of advice, young man," Ed Dedalus told Johnny. "Sunny Biggs is the star here. You are just a minor moon."

"What is that supposed to mean?" Johnny asked.

"Don't fly too high, kid," Dedalus said. "Don't get too close to the Sun Man. You'll get burned."

Model

Twenty people paid a total of $540 to get tickets for Johnny's show. How much did each ticket cost?

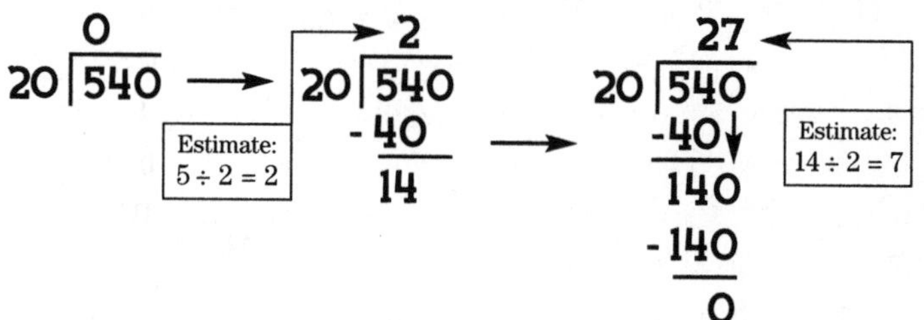

How many times does 20 go into 5? It doesn't, so move on.	How many times does 20 go into 54? Estimate by asking: *How many times does 2 go into 5?*	How many times does 20 go into 140? Estimate: *How many 2's are in 14?*

Find each quotient. Some answers may have a remainder.

1. $20\overline{)360}$

2. $30\overline{)150}$

3. $40\overline{)560}$

4. $70\overline{)910}$

5. $30\overline{)965}$

6. $50\overline{)232}$

2-Digit Division

Name ______________________ **Date** ______________

But Johnny didn't listen. In fact, he decided to put on a new, more spectacular show right across the street from Sunny's show.

"That's too close," Dedalus told Johnny. "Don't get too close to the Sun Man."

But Johnny—who now billed himself as *Icarus*—not only did it. He got a new costume—even more spectacular than Sunny's. It was shaped like a huge bird, and had gigantic wax wings to make Johnny seem like some magnificent creature floating over the stage.

"I'm telling you, kid," Dedalus said. "Don't do it. Don't get too close to Sunny. You'll get burned."

The night of Johnny's first show came. Wearing his spectacular wax bird costume, Icarus swooped down on the stage. "This is great!" the audience cried. "This is fabulous. This is better than Sunny!"

Model

There were 736 people in the audience at Johnny's show. They sat in 32 rows. How many people sat in each row?

```
    0              2               23
32)736         32)736          32)736
                  -64             -64↓
                    9               96
                                   -96
                                     0
```

Estimate: 7 ÷ 3 = 2

Estimate: 9 ÷ 3 = 3

How many times does 32 go into 7? It doesn't, so move on.

How many times does 32 go into 73? Estimate by asking: ***How many times does 3 go into 7?***

How many times does 32 go into 96? Estimate: ***How many 3's are in 9?***

Find each quotient.

7. $13\overline{)273}$

8. $22\overline{)792}$

9. $29\overline{)493}$

10. $41\overline{)820}$

11. $53\overline{)1431}$

12. $48\overline{)1488}$

Icarus kept playing. "GO, JOHNNY, GO!" they cried.

But then the bright hot lights started to take effect. Johnny's spectacular wax bird costume began to melt. Soon, Icarus was falling apart, his bird costume drooping into a weeping, gooey mess!

"BOO!" the audience cried.

Icarus tried to keep playing, but it was no use. His show was crashing to the ground and there was nothing he could do about it. The audience got up to leave.

"Let's go over and see Sunny," they said.

To make a long story short, that was the end of Johnny Icarus. At least in Vegas. Oh, he still plays and everything, but it's strictly small-time stuff. Today, Johnny admits it himself.

"I got too close to the Sun," he says. "I learned my lesson. The hard way."

THE END

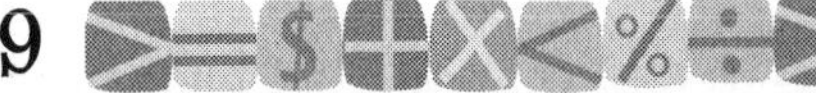

Name ________________________ Date ____________

The Magic Dancing Shoes

Anya loved dancing. Every afternoon she stood at the window of Slick Arnold's Dance Studio and stared inside at the dancers.

"If only I could be like them," Anya sighed.

One day, Slick Arnold noticed her. "Hey kid," he said. "Why don't you come in and learn to dance? Your first lesson is only $19.95 plus shipping and handling."

"Shipping and handling?" Anya said. "Why would I need shipping and handling when I'm standing right here?"

"Good question," said Slick Arnold, who was nothing if he wasn't slick. "I tell you what, kid. I'll *drop* the shipping and handling charge if you sign up right now for the full 9-week course. That's a $1253 value for $126. *Plus* I'll throw in two BONUS lessons for an additional $171, including tax, title, and destination fee."

Model

How much will the 9-week course cost per week if Anya signs up for bonus lessons? First calculate the total.

$$\begin{array}{r} 126 \\ +\,171 \\ \hline 297 \end{array}$$

Then, divide by 9, the number of weeks for the course:

$$\begin{array}{r} 33 \\ 9\overline{)297} \\ -27\downarrow \\ \hline 27 \\ -27 \\ \hline 0 \end{array}$$

____

Calculate. Round your answer to the nearest whole when necessary.

1. How much will the 9-week course cost per week if Anya does *not* sign up for bonus lessons?

   ____

2. How much would the course cost each week if Anya paid the regular price?

   ____

3. Without the bonus lessons, how much does Anya save over the regular $1253 price for the course?

   ____

4. How much will Anya save each week?

   ____

5. If Anya buys Arnold's 9-week special without the bonus lessons, how much is the average daily cost?

   ____

"That's a mighty attractive offer, Mr. Arnold," Anya said meekly. "But I couldn't. I'm just too clumsy and awkward to be a dancer."

Slick Arnold took Anya by the arm. He showed her pictures on the wall of famous dancers Murph Bunsen and Pebble Pearson.

"Wow," Anya said. "Murph and Pebble. Did you teach *them* how to dance?"

Slick Arnold shook his head. "Not exactly," he said. "But the point is, they were just like you: shy, awkward, and clumsy. They claimed they couldn't do it. But they had one thing you don't have."

Fractured Fairy Tales Multiplication & Division • Scholastic Teaching Resources

Name ______________________________ **Date** ______________

"What's that?" Anya asked.

Slick Arnold reached into a closet and pulled out a box.

"A pair of Magic Dancing Shoes," he said. "You put them on, then bingo! You're a great dancer! And all for a low, low price of $116 in 6 easy payments."

"It's as easy as that?" Anya said.

"Even easier," Slick Arnold said. "Because right now, I can let you have the shoes, the 9-week course, the bonus lessons, plus my own Slick Arnold CD *Dance Machine*, all for the unheard of price of 18 easy installment payments of $36 each. What do you say, kid?"

6. What is the total cost of the installment payments for the complete package?

____

7. Slick Arnold will lower each payment to $26 if Anya makes 27 installment payments instead of 18. Is this a good deal? How much more or less will Anya pay for this deal?

____

8. Slick Arnold sold 35 dance courses for $171 each, and 13 courses for $126 each. How much did he make in all?

____

The rest, as they say, is history. Anya bought the Magic Dancing Shoes, the 9-week course, the bonus lessons, and the CD—all for Slick Arnold's low, low price. And the next day she showed up at Slick Arnold's Dance Studio and started to learn to dance.

And she wasn't too bad, either.

Did the Magic Dancing Shoes help?

"Hey, they couldn't hurt," said Slick Arnold.

THE END

Name ______________________ Date ____________

Jack and the Magic Beans, Part 1

Jack lived with his mother and they were poor. To get money, Jack's mother sent him to Sharky's Used Car Lot to sell their car, a rusty '98 Road Cow with more than 200,000 miles on it. The Road Cow had little value, but when Jack traded it in for a handful of "magic" beans, his mother was furious.

"Magic, *shmagic*!" she cried.

And she threw the beans out the window.

The next morning, when Jack looked out the window there was no magic beanstalk. But there was a high-rise out there, known as the Beanstalk Building.

Jack found the magic beans where his mother had thrown them—on the sidewalk in front of the new building. He took them inside, roasted them to a dark, glossy sheen and brewed them with milk into a delicious hot drink.

"I think I'll call this *cappuccino*!" Jack said.

Needless to say, the drink caught on. Soon Jack had turned their cottage into a swank café named Jack's. Jack's did great business. And because the beans were magic, Jack never seemed to run out of them.

Model

One reason Jack did so well was that he used mental math in his business. For example, if 10 people ordered double-lattés for \$3.25, Jack would multiply by 10 moving the decimal point one place to the right.

\$3.25 x 10 → move one place right = \$32.50

Use mental math to find each product.

1. \$0.49 x 10 → move one place right = ________
2. \$1.69 x 10 → move one place right = ________
3. \$0.21 x 10 → move one place right = ________
4. \$12.19 x 10 → move one place right = ________
5. \$341.75 x 10 = ________

Model

To multiply by 100 he moved the decimal *two* places to the right.

\$3.25 x 100 → move two places right = \$325.00

\$0.53 x 100 → move two places right = \$53.00

6. 0.531 x 100 → move two places right = ______
7. \$6.50 x 100 → move two places right = ______
8. 24.63 x 100 → move two places right = ______
9. 0.076 x 100 → move two places right = ______
10. \$45.12 x 100 → move two places right = ______

Decimal Multiplication

Name ______________________________ **Date** ______________

The café was so successful that a second coffee shop soon sprang up to catch some of Jack's overflow business. This café was owned by a giant—Chuck Giant was his name. He called the place Giant's Sky Café. The Sky Café was located on the top floor of the Beanstalk Building.

Chuck Giant was a well-known bad guy. Giant was bitterly jealous of Jack's café. His own coffee was bad; it tasted like dishwater.

"If only I had those magic beans," Giant was often heard to mutter.

One morning Jack woke up and his magic beans were gone! Normally, he kept them inside of a ceramic golden goose—but suddenly, the goose was nowhere to be found!

By some coincidence, word got out that the coffee at Giant's Sky Café was suddenly improved. Indeed, Giant's espresso was now excellent! Its cappuccino was colossal! Its latté was luscious!

Needless to say, Jack was suspicious. Had giant taken the magic beans? There was only one way to find out!

End of Part 1. See Part 2 for the thrilling conclusion of this story!

Use mental math to find each product.

11. 63.7 x 10 = _______

12. 65.22 x 100 = _______

13. 17.09 x 10 = _______

14. $56.12 x 100 = _______

15. 525.4 x 10 = _______

16. 14.39 x 100 = _______

17. To make one cup of coffee, Jack needs 4.3 ounces of water. How much water does he need to make 10 cups?

____

18. Jack makes a $0.47 profit on each cup of cappuccino he sells. How much profit does he make on 100 cups of cappuccino?

____

Name ______________________ Date ____________

Jack and the Magic Beans, Part 2

Our story so far: *Jack traded in the family car for magic beans. He used the beans to open his café, Jack's. His café was a success but the café in the nearby Beanstalk Building owned by a well-known bad guy, Chuck Giant, was not a success. Giant was extremely jealous of Jack and the magic beans that Jack kept in a golden goose. One morning Jack discovered the golden goose was gone!*

Jack was determined to get the golden goose back. But when he came to the Beanstalk Building, the elevators were out of order.

Now there was only one way to get to the top of the Beanstalk Building—Jack would need to climb there!

So climb he did. On the 44th floor, Jack finally reached the Sky Café. He tumbled in through the window and immediately hid.

Now Giant had a good nose, and he instantly said: "Fee, fie, foe, fum, I smell a cup of English-One!"

English-One was a type of tea Jack had been making that morning (because he was out of coffee beans). It was a soothing blend that was known to put people to sleep. Giant asked Wanda, Giant's kindly waitress, to bring him a cup of the tea, and he quickly fell asleep. At this point, Jack rushed out.

"Quick!" he said to Wanda. "Where is the golden goose?"

Now Wanda was a good person, and she hated working for Giant, who was cruel, dishonest, and stole most of her tips. So she gave Jack the golden goose with the magic beans inside.

Model

Wanda had to divide up \$64.80 in tips among 10 different people. She did this mentally by moving the decimal point one place to the left. You can, too.

\$64.80 ÷ 10 → move one place left = \$6.48
576.87 ÷ 10 → move one place left = 57.687

1. \$8.80 ÷ 10 → move one place left = _______

2. 44.31 ÷ 10 → move one place left = _______

3. 168.1 ÷ 10 → move one place left = _______

4. 5.5 ÷ 10 → move one place left = _______

Name ______________________________ Date ______________

Model

To divide by 100 he moved the decimal *two* places.
$4643.00 ÷ 100 → move two places to the left
= $46.43

5. 118.78 ÷ 100 → move two places left = _______

6. $62.00 ÷ 100 → move two places left = _______

7. 255.6 ÷ 100 → move two places left = _______

8. 8257.4 ÷ 100 → move two places left = _______

"I've got to go," Jack said, as soon as he had the beans.

"I'll go with you!" cried Wanda.

So the two of them escaped. Jack went back to his café. Wanda joined him as his new business manager. With his golden goose full of magic beans back, Jack's was busier and better than ever. And Giant? He was ruined. He lost his lease on the Giant's Sky Café and had to go back to his rodent extermination business.

A few years later Jack sold Jack's café to a large corporation. Jack, Wanda, and Jack's mother currently live in Florida, where they head the Magic Bean Foundation, an organization dedicated to helping people avoid getting swindled when they trade in used cars.

THE END

Use mental math to find each quotient.

9. $78.30 ÷ 10 = _______

10. 912.3 ÷ 10 = _______

11. 65.22 ÷ 100 = _______

12. 441.67 ÷ 100 = _______

13. 29.43 ÷ 100 = _______

14. 872.3 ÷ 10 = _______

15. 66.22 ÷ 10 = _______

16. 5.9 ÷ 100 = _______

17. The Magic Bean Foundation collected $8759 from 10 donors. What was the average amount that each donor gave?

____

18. The Magic Bean Foundation plans to use the $8759 it collected to help 100 people. On the average, how much money will each person get?

____

Name ______________________________ Date ______________

The Fisherman and His Fish

On a bright and sunny day, a fisherman threw his line into the water and hooked a large and beautiful fish.

"Please let me go," said the fish. "For I am no ordinary fish. I am actually a lovely princess who has been enchanted by an evil sorcerer."

"I am no ordinary fisherman myself," said the fisherman. "I'm about to be a bridegroom. Tomorrow, I'm getting married!"

"Ooh, a wedding," said the fish. "I love weddings. Take me with you, fisherman."

So the fisherman brought the fish to his wedding. His bride-to-be wasn't pleased.

"I don't care *who* you say she is," his fiancée said. "Get rid of her. I don't want some fish messing up my wedding."

This comment revealed the true character of his wife-to-be. She was not a nice person and now the fisherman knew for sure.

"Don't worry," he said to his fiancée. "This fish won't ruin our wedding because there isn't going to *be* any wedding. I'm canceling it right now."

"You can't do that!" screeched the bride-to-be.

But the fisherman did do it. The wedding was called off. The guests went home.

Afterward, the fisherman found himself alone with his fish.

"Would you like to have dinner?" he asked.

"I'd love to," said the fish.

Model

The wedding planner had arranged for 8 guests to sit at each table. Each guest would have been served 4.35 ounces of sparkling water. How many ounces would the guests at each table have had to drink in all?

$\begin{array}{r} {}^{2}4.{}^{4}35 \\ \times\ 8 \\ \hline 3480 \end{array}$	$\begin{array}{r} 4.35 \\ \times\ 8 \\ \hline \end{array}$	$\begin{array}{r} 4.35 \\ \times\ 8 \\ \hline 34.80 \end{array}$
Multiply as you would with whole numbers.	Count the decimal places: 2	Move the decimal point left the same number of places.

Find each product.

1. $\begin{array}{r} 3.4 \\ \times\ 3 \\ \hline \end{array}$

2. $\begin{array}{r} 4.2 \\ \times\ 3 \\ \hline \end{array}$

3. $\begin{array}{r} 0.14 \\ \times\ 14 \\ \hline \end{array}$

4. $\begin{array}{r} 4.76 \\ \times\ 33 \\ \hline \end{array}$

5. $\begin{array}{r} 73.1 \\ \times\ 24 \\ \hline \end{array}$

6. $\begin{array}{r} 4.25 \\ \times\ 34 \\ \hline \end{array}$

Name ______________________ **Date** ______________

7. 53 x .43

8. 8.05 x 69

9. 30.9 x 81

10. 0.81 x 46

11. 90.2 x 74

12. 48.9 x 35

They went to a restaurant. "Do you serve seafood here?" the fisherman asked the waiter once they were seated.

"Yes, we do," said the waiter.

It was a lovely meal. The fisherman and the fish talked for hours about everything under the sun. After dinner they went to the river and in the moonlight looked into each other's eyes.

Could I be falling in love with a fish? the fisherman thought to himself.

Should I tell him the truth? the fish thought to herself.

"I was thinking," said the fisherman, "that after you turn into a princess again I would ask you to marry me. Is that too much to ask?"

"Yes," said the fish, "for I have a confession to make. I am not really a princess. I'm a fish through and through. I'll *never* turn back into a princess because I never *was* a princess in the first place."

The fisherman could not speak. It was true that the fish was a noble and beautiful creature. But she *was*, after all, a fish. Could he spend the rest of his life with a *fish*?

Fortunately, he never had to answer that question. At that moment, his ex-fiancée appeared.

The fisherman had always suspected that there was something odd about her. Now he knew what it was:

"You're an evil sorceress!" he cried.

"You're right," she said. "And since you refused to marry me I have no choice but pay you back," said the fiancée.

And with that, she turned the fisherman into a rainbow trout. He and the fish then jumped in the water and were never heard from again.

THE END

Model

The sorceress usually charged 8.5 silver ducats for each minute she worked. If it took 7.25 minutes to cast a spell, how much did she charge?

${}^{2}7.{}^{4}25$ x 8.5 3625 58000 61625	7.25 x 8.5	7.25 x 8.5 61.625
Multiply as you would with whole numbers.	**Count decimal places: 3**	**Move the decimal point left the same number of places.**

Find each product.

13. 2.3 x 2.5

14. 5.2 x 1.6

15. 0.14 x 0.3

16. 5.27 x 2.3

Name ______________________ Date ____________

The Elves and the Screenwriter

Once there was a humble screenwriter named Vida who toiled all day on her laptop writing screenplays. She was good at character and story, but her action scenes were often weak.

Indeed, Morty, Vida's agent, complained bitterly. "For goodness sake, Vida," he said one day. "Would it kill you to put in a few car chases and other action scenes?"

"But it'll ruin the story," insisted Vida.

That night Vida worked for hours on her new script. She worked so hard that she finally fell asleep at her desk. When she awoke the next morning, she looked at her script, and lo and behold—something amazing had occurred! Someone had inserted several car chases and other action scenes into the story.

At first Vida was angry. But when she showed the work to Morty, he was delighted.

"This is great stuff, kid!" Morty cried. "Fabulous! Great action!"

And sure enough, that very same day Morty sold the script to a studio for a nice chunk of change. Vida was thrilled. It was her first big sale.

Model

Vida divided her 94.2-page long screenplay into 6 sections of equal length. How long is each section?

$90 \div 6 \approx 10–20 \longrightarrow 6\overline{)94.2} \longrightarrow$

```
   15.7
6 )94.2
   -6
   34
  -30
    42
   -42
     0
```

Make a rough estimate: the quotient is between 10 and 20	Move the decimal place up.	Divide as you would with whole numbers

Find each quotient.

1. $3\overline{)25.2}$

2. $2\overline{)9.2}$

3. $4\overline{)52.4}$

4. $8\overline{)155.2}$

5. $5\overline{)8.85}$

6. $2\overline{)1.44}$

7. $6\overline{)169.92}$

8. $5\overline{)19.35}$

Name ______________________________ Date ________________

Vida began working on a new screenplay the next day. Once again, she fell asleep and when she awoke she found new action scenes inserted into her script.

"What's going on here?" Vida asked herself.

That night, Vida was determined to find out who was changing her script. So she set her alarm. At 3:00 A.M., Vida awoke to find two of the cutest creatures you ever did see pecking away at her laptop, inserting chase scenes and wild special effects into her script.

"Who are you?" Vida asked.

"We're elves," they said.

"No, you're not," Vida said. "There's no such thing as elves. Who are you really?"

"Yes, we are" they insisted. "We're not only elves. We're professional script doctors. We were hired by an unnamed friend to fix your screenplay."

Vida began to ponder who this unnamed friend might be. The next morning she confessed to Morty.

He confessed, as well. "It was me, sweetheart," said Morty. "I hope you don't mind. I knew you wouldn't go along with the 'script doctor' idea, so I sort of took it upon myself. Sorry."

"No need to say you're sorry," Vida said. "Because you're fired."

"You're kidding, right?" Morty said.

Vida smiled. "Yes, I'm kidding. You've convinced me, Morty. If they want *action* in their scripts, we might as well give it to them."

So they became a successful screenwriting team—Vida and the two elves—and they lived happily ever after.

THE END

Model

The special effects team for Vida's movie created 20 explosions using 3.24 pounds of explosive material. How much material did they use for each explosion?

$$20\overline{)3.24}$$

$$\begin{array}{r} .16 \\ 20\overline{)3.24} \\ -20\downarrow \\ \hline 124 \\ -120 \\ \hline 4 \end{array} \quad \longrightarrow \quad \begin{array}{r} .162 \\ 20\overline{)3.240} \\ -20 \\ \hline 124 \\ -120\downarrow \\ \hline 40 \\ -40 \\ \hline 0 \end{array}$$

First pull up the decimal point. Then estimate. The quotient will be smaller than 1.

Rather than write "4" as a remainder, keep going.

Attach a zero. Then finish the problem.

Find each quotient.

9. $10\overline{)4.93}$

10. $20\overline{)9.36}$

11. $50\overline{)66.05}$

12. $43\overline{)10.234}$

13. $60\overline{)26.58}$

14. $32\overline{)2.704}$

Name ______________________ Date ____________

King Vitas and the Fraction Touch

The kingdom of King Vitas enjoyed a strong economy, low unemployment, and had lots of goats. In fact, the GDP (Goat Domestic Product) of Vitas's kingdom was number one in the region. It was often said that the only things Vitas really cared about were his goats.

Then one day a traveler came to the kingdom with a special offer.

"If you sell me your finest goat," the traveler told the king, "I will grant you one wish."

"I don't want any wishes," said Vitas. "I just want my goats."

But the traveler (who didn't listen so well) said, "All right, from now on, everything you touch will turn to gold."

Vitas touched a leaf. It turned to gold. He touched a sandwich. It also turned to gold. He touched bucket. It too turned to gold.

"Isn't that great?" said the traveler.

"No, I hate it," said Vitas. "I'll do anything to get rid of this Golden Touch."

"*Anything?*" said the traveler. "Even sell me your favorite goat?"

"Yes," said King Vitas. But when it was time to hand the goat over, Vitas changed his mind and gave the traveler a lesser goat.

Model

The King's special collection included 12 goats. Three-fourths of these goats were prize-winners. How many goats were prize-winners?

$\frac{3}{4} \times 12 = \frac{3}{4} \times \frac{12}{1} \rightarrow \frac{3}{4} \times \frac{12}{1} = \frac{36}{4} = 9$

Write each number as a fraction. Multiply, then simplify.

Find each product.

1. $\frac{1}{3} \times 6$
2. $\frac{1}{2} \times 14$
3. $\frac{1}{6} \times 12$
4. $\frac{1}{5} \times 20$
5. $\frac{2}{3} \times 12$
6. $\frac{2}{5} \times 10$
7. $\frac{3}{7} \times 21$
8. $\frac{2}{9} \times 18$
9. $\frac{3}{5} \times 30$
10. $\frac{5}{8} \times 40$

Name ______________________________ **Date** ______________

When he saw the lesser goat, the traveler was furious. So now he gave Vitas a new "Stone Touch." Everything Vitas touched turned to stone: a comb, a book, a nut, a flower.

"Please," said King Vitas. "Take away this Stone Touch. I'll give you my finest goat. I promise."

So the deal was made, but once again Vitas didn't follow through. So the traveler now gave Vitas the Wooden Touch. Everything he touched turned to wood.

Vitas didn't hold on this deal either, so the pattern continued. From then on King Vitas had in order: the Iron Touch, the Leather Touch, the Formica Touch, the Barbecue Sauce Touch, and many other "touches."

Finally, King Vitas asked to speak plainly with the traveler.

"Who are you?" he asked.

"I come from Mt. Olympus," said the traveler. "I represent some very important individuals there. I their Chief Goat-Buyer. I have been sent here to obtain your best goat."

"Wow!" thought Vitas, "Mt. Olympus!"

But he still could not part with his best goat. So they compromised. In exchange for his second-best goat, Vitas would receive the Fraction Touch. It allowed Vitas to reduce anything he touched to a fraction of its size.

"The Fraction Touch?" said Vitas. "How will I ever use that?"

"It comes in handy," said the Goat-Buyer. "You'll be surprised."

And surprised he was. Fractions were quite useful, Vitas discovered.

And from then on King Vitas was known as the "King with the Fraction Touch."

So if you ever have any problems with fractions—or goats—you know where to go.

THE END

Model

King Vitas used the Fraction Touch to shrink half of a melon to $\frac{2}{3}$ of its size. What fraction of a melon did he end up with?

$$\frac{1}{\cancel{2}_1} \times \frac{\cancel{2}^1}{3} = \frac{1}{3}$$

If possible, simplify before you multiply to make the problem easier.

Find each product.

11. $\frac{4}{7} \times 21$

12. $\frac{5}{6} \times 9$

13. $\frac{1}{2} \times \frac{1}{2}$

14. $\frac{2}{3} \times \frac{1}{4}$

15. $\frac{1}{4} \times \frac{3}{8}$

16. $\frac{3}{5} \times \frac{5}{8}$

17. $\frac{4}{5} \times \frac{1}{2}$

18. $\frac{1}{3} \times \frac{6}{7}$

19. $\frac{7}{8} \times \frac{4}{21}$

20. $\frac{4}{5} \times \frac{5}{7}$

Fractured Fairy Tales Multiplication & Division • Scholastic Teaching Resources

Name ______________________________ Date ______________

The Duck Puppy

Young Prince Arthur always got what he wanted. There were three things he wanted for his birthday: a book, a whistle, and a puppy. Minister Rowena was sent out to get them. She had no trouble finding the book and the whistle. But when she went to the pet shop they said: "Sorry, no puppies."

"You don't understand," Rowena told the shopkeeper. "This puppy is for the young prince, and the young prince ALWAYS gets what he wants."

"I have a duck," the shopkeeper said.

So Rowena bought the duck, wrapped it as a gift, and returned just in time for the party. It was a splendid party. The prince blew out the candles and opened his gifts.

All went well until the final gift. The prince took off the wrapping paper and out popped the duck instead of a puppy.

"Are you *sure* this is a puppy?" the prince asked, looking suspiciously at his gift.

"Of course," Rowena said. "It's a special kind of puppy. You'll love this puppy. I guarantee it."

And indeed, Young Prince Arthur really did love his "puppy." And he treated the duck just like a puppy, too. He put a collar around its neck. He took it for walks on a leash. He fed it gourmet puppy food.

And he named it, well, Puppy.

In fact, as time passed everyone in the castle became fond of the prince's "puppy." Which put them all in a panic when one day Puppy took it in its mind to *fly* over the castle wall.

"Puppy is lost!" cried the prince. "Call the sheriff!"

The sheriff, who knew nothing about the situation, was summoned.

"Can you describe this puppy?" the sheriff asked.

"Puppy is green and white," the prince told him. "He has webbed feet, a long orange bill, and dark feathers."

"A green and white puppy?" cried the sheriff. "With dark feathers and webbed feet? That doesn't sound like a puppy to me. That sounds like a—"

At that very moment—just in the nick of time—the animal came hurtling across the wall.

"Puppy!" cried the prince. "You've come home to me. Good dog! Good dog!"

Rowena and the sheriff left the young boy to be with his cherished pet. The sheriff could only shake his head in disbelief.

"Well, you know what they say," Rowena said to the sheriff. "If it looks like a duck, and it walks like a duck, and it talks like a duck . . ."

"Then what?" the sheriff asked.

"Then it's a puppy," Rowena said.

THE END

Name ______________________ Date ____________

Model

It took Puppy 24 days to eat an 864 ounce bag of gourmet dog food. How much food did Puppy eat on an average day?
Answer: 3.6 ounces

```
     3.6
24 | 86.4
    -72↓
     144
    -144
       0
```

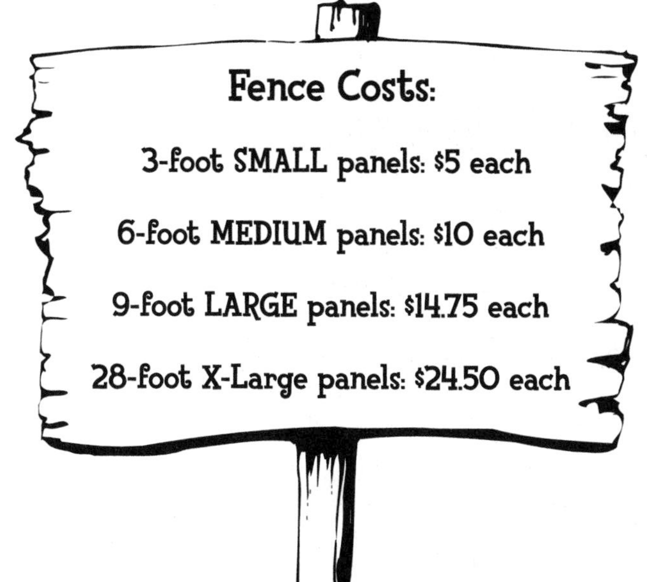

Calculate.

1. The prince served Royal Jug Juice at his party from a 30-ounce jug. The prince insisted that each guest be served 7 full ounces of juice. How many jugs were needed for 13 guests? How much juice would be left over?

____

2. If 13 guests had one 7-ounce glass of juice, and 6 guests had a second glass, how many 30-ounce jugs of juice would be needed? How many guests could have a third glass of juice?

____

3. For next year's party, the prince plans to invite 23 guests and serve 8-ounce glasses of juice. How many 30-ounce jugs will he need to serve one glass to each guest?

____

4. Rowena wants to build a rectangular fenced-in pen for Puppy that measures 27 feet by 12 feet. Which combination of fence panels should she buy if she wants to spend as little money as possible? How much will she spend?

____

____

____

5. In problem 4, how much will Rowena spend if she buys 28-foot panels only and cuts them down to size? How many extra feet of fencing will she have?

____

____

____

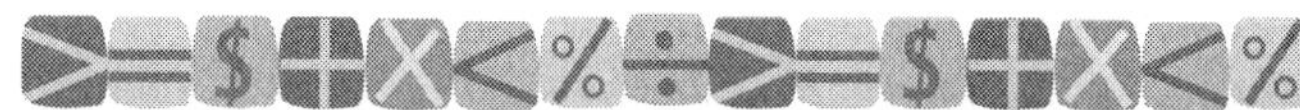

Fractured Fairy Tales Multiplication & Division • Scholastic Teaching Resources

Name ______________________________ Date ______________

The Leap Frogs

Three Leap Frogs in the pond argued about who could jump the farthest. Along came a king who said, "Whosoever can jump farthest will win my daughter's hand in marriage."

So a Royal Leaping Contest was organized. The contestants all lined up outside the Royal Leaping Box.

The first frog up leaped so far that he went outside of the Leaping Box, over the trees and into the stables.

The leap was so far out of bounds that the judges did not know how to measure it.

The second frog also leaped far. In fact, this fellow leaped out of the box and right into the lap of the Princess, splashing her with pond slime, which did not please her one bit.

The third frog was in fact was not a Leap Frog at all, but a Hopping Toad, and a rather dull one at that. The Hopping Toad gave more of a hop than a leap, jumping just a few inches and staying well inside of the Leaping Box.

Now the judges had to declare a winner. The first Leap Frog, they decided, had made a fine jump, but it was definitely outside of the box.

So that wouldn't do.

The second frog's jump was also impressive. But he too had gone outside of the box—plus he had upset the Princess by splashing her with slime.

So that wouldn't do either.

The third frog—or rather the Toad—had not jumped far, but he had at least stayed inside of the boundaries.

So the Toad was declared the winner.

Everyone was unhappy with the decision. Everyone complained, except for the Toad. He soon turned into a handsome prince, but when he came to claim the hand of the Princess, she promptly turned him down.

"I'll find my own husband, if you don't mind," she said.

So in the end, no one was satisfied—not the frogs, not the Toad, and not the princess either.

By and by, the Toad, who was now a handsome prince, applied for a job as a Royal Advisor, but was turned down because, as the king said, he was unable to function "outside of the box."

The Princess? She married the Jester, but the two were divorced three years later because she couldn't stand his constant joking and chuckling.

No one lived happily ever after.

THE END

Name ______________________________ Date ______________

Model

The regulation leaping box measured 42.4 feet by 25.7 feet. What was the perimeter of the box?

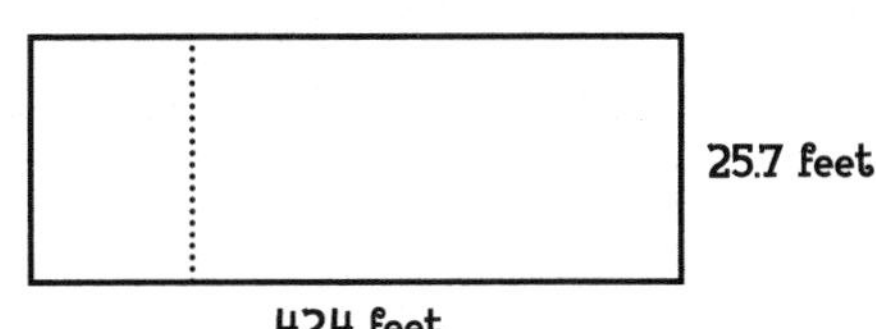

Answer: 136.2 feet

1. To warm up, the first Leap Frog ran around the outside of the box 4.5 times. How far did he run?

2. What was the area of the box?

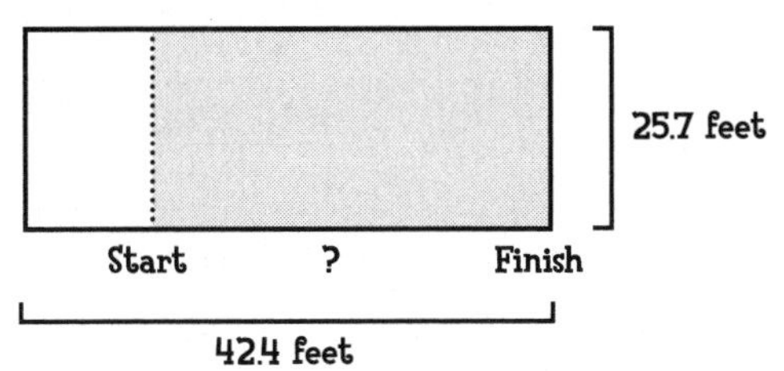

3. The Start and Finish lines are shown. The Start line is 10.6 feet from the edge of the leaping box. What is the distance from the Start to the Finish line?

4. What is the area of the shaded portion of the leaping box?

5. If the box were widened by 4.3 feet and lengthened by 3.4 feet. What would its perimeter be?

6. What would the area of this larger leaping box be?

7. The viewing area has a perimeter of 58.6 feet. It is 12.5 feet wide. What is its length?

8. The snack bar covers an area of 210 square feet. It is 15 feet wide. What is its length?

9. If a square has a perimeter of 32 feet and an area of 64 square feet, how long are each of its sides?

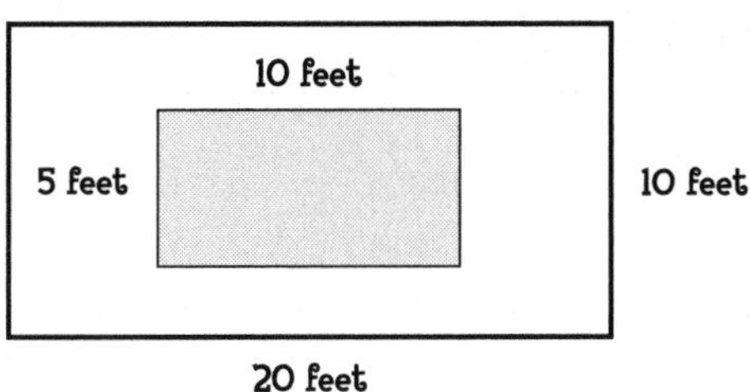

10. The prince has ordered a fence to be put around the perimeter of both the outer and inner areas of the castle courtyard. Using the measurements above, how many feet of fencing will he need?

Name ______________________________ **Date** ______________

Modern Medieval Science Magazine

Table of Contents

How do we know Earth is flat? Try this experiment: Put a round ball on the ground. Does it roll away? No. "This *proves* that Earth is flat," says scientist Lobar the Certain. Also, Lobar points out two other key reasons why Earth must be flat: (1) The king says so. (2) Whatever the king says is true.

For years scientists have said that there are four elements: earth, wind, fire, and water. Now a fifth element may have been discovered: mud. "If you stir all of the other elements together," says alchemist Jenny the Soupmaker, "you get a mixture that's much like mud. So it must be an element, too."

Alchemists working at the Center for Ignorance Is Bliss reported making 8 ounces of pure gold from 5 ounces of tin and 3 ounces of lead. "This is exciting!" said lead chemist, Sasha the Deluded. The experimenters note that they did need to use the 9 ounces of "starter" gold to get the experiment going.

That's right, that bath you took last August may actually be good for your health, claims health expert Mongo the Meek. "It gets rid of rodents and other pests," Mongo says. "Just make sure you don't overdue it," he adds. "One bath a year should do it, ideally during the warm summer months."

When you go for a "leech treatment" you may think the leeches are all alike. "Not true!" says leech expert, Billy the Jolly Barber. In fact, "Some leeches are happier than others and do a better job of sucking your blood," Billy claims. How can you tell them apart? "Look for leeches with little smiles on their faces," Billy says. "It's a tell-tale sign that you've got the best leeches money can buy."

The king's new calculator is the very latest in modern technology. The new calculator is named Doris and she can perform almost 7 calculations per minute.* Doris replaces the king's old calculator, an early model named Walter who rarely performed over 2 calculations per minute and was reported to have taken "way too many bathroom breaks."

* If you give her a proper lunchbreak and the calculations, according to Doris, "are not too hard."

Using a Calculator

Name ______________________________ Date ______________

Model

The King's new calculator gives the product of 333.25 and 9.876 as 3291.177. Is this answer correct? Use your own calculator to check the sum.

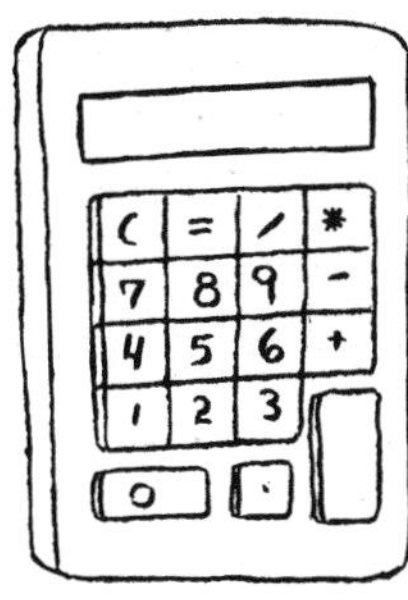

____

Solve these problems with a calculator.

1. 11.99 x 15.01 = _______

2. 149.40875 ÷ 5.97635 = _______

3. 938.2 + 458.32 ÷ 139.652 = _______

4. 88.2 - 15.69 - 4.99 x 4.99 = _______

5. 617.4 x 3.789 = _______

6. 110 x 35.444 + 2798 = _______

7. 0.175 x 0.55 - 0.005 + 0.222 = _______

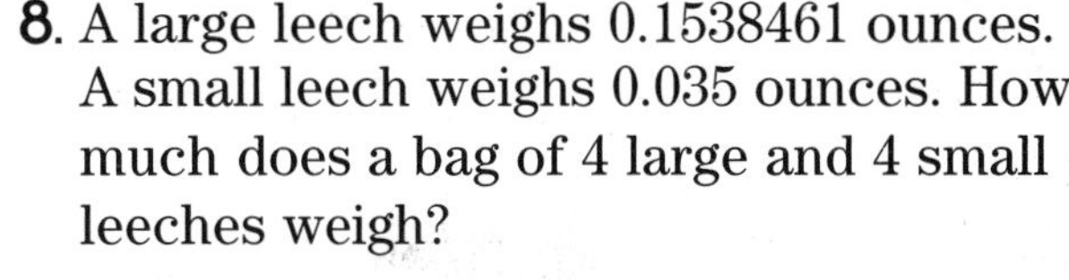

8. A large leech weighs 0.1538461 ounces. A small leech weighs 0.035 ounces. How much does a bag of 4 large and 4 small leeches weigh?

____

9. Jenny the Soupmaker reports that a spark weighs 0.09332 ounces. If you put together 12 sparks, you get a fire. How much would this fire weigh, according to Jenny's way of calculating?

____

10. Lobar the Certain divided his flat Earth map into sectors that were 354.875 miles wide. If there were 24 of these sectors, how wide was the entire Earth, according to Lobar?

____

11. The dragon's bath water cooled from 210.47 degrees to 176.5714 degrees. By how many degrees did it cool?

____

Name ______________________________ Date ______________

The Four Beautiful Ducklings

Mother Duck laid four beautiful eggs that soon hatched into four beautiful young ducklings. As it turned out, the four ducklings were quite competitive. They were constantly trying to outdo each other to see who was best. They had swimming races. They had flapping races. They had running races and worm-finding contests.

One day they got to talking about which duckling was Mother Duck's favorite.

"I am!" cried the first duckling. "Because I'm the best swimmer."

"No, I am!" said the second duckling. "Because I'm the best flapper."

"I am!" said the third duckling. "Because I'm the best runner and worm-finder."

"No, I'm her favorite!" cried the fourth duckling. "Because I'm not the best at anything, so she feels sorry for me."

It wasn't long before the first duckling went to Mother Duck and asked, "Who is your favorite duckling?"

"Why you are, first duckling," said Mother Duck. "Because you're the best swimmer."

And she gave him a secret blue pebble to show that he would always be her favorite.

"Never show this to anyone," said Mother Duck.

Soon the second duckling came with the same question. This time, Mother Duck said that *she* was the favorite, because she was the best flapper. And she gave a secret blue pebble to this second duckling as well.

"Thank you," said the second duckling. "I'll never show this to anyone."

After that, the third duckling came. She was followed by the fourth duckling. Each was told that he or she was Mother Duck's favorite. And they each received a secret blue pebble and were told that they should never show it to anyone or tell anyone about it.

By and by, the ducklings began to compare stories and found out that Mother Duck had named *each* of them as her favorite. So they went to Mother Duck.

"You told the first duckling that he was the favorite because he was such a good swimmer," they said.

"That's true," said Mother Duck.

"You told the second duckling that she was the favorite because she was such a good flapper," they said.

"That's also true," said Mother Duck.

And so it went with the third and fourth ducklings. They, too, had been told that they were the favorites.

"I must admit," said Mother Duck, "I did say all of that."

"Well which is it?" the ducklings asked. "We can't *ALL* be the favorite."

"Ah," said Mother Duck. "Here I hope that whomever I name is able to keep a secret."

"Of course we can keep a secret," said the ducklings. "We promise!"

"Then my answer to you is this," said Mother Duck. "My one true favorite is the one I gave the secret blue pebble to. You know who you are."

"Aha," said all four ducklings quietly.

And they all went off in their own ways, each satisfied that the secret would never be revealed.

Multistep Word Problems

Name ______________________ **Date** __________

Model

In the lake, Mother Duck swam 46 feet from the shore to the dock. Then she swam 83 feet to the reeds. From the reeds, she swam 67 feet back to the dock. If she made this same round trip 6 times, how far did she travel in all?

First add to find the total of one trip:
46 + 83 + 67 = 196 feet
Then multiply to find the total distance:
196 x 6 = 1176 feet

---

1. The four eggs that Mother Duck laid each took 4 weeks and 4 days to hatch. In all, how many days did the eggs take to hatch?

   ____

2. In the swimming race, the first duckling swam at a rate of 3 feet per second. How long would it take him to swim from one side of a 48-foot wide pond to the other, and back again?

   ____

3. The second duckling flew 126 yards to the old tree. Then she flew 43 yards to the old stone fence. Then she flew 55 yards back to the old tree. It took a total of 16 seconds to make this trip. How fast was the duckling moving?

   ____

4. In the worm-finding contest, the first duckling found 13 worms. The second duckling found 4 times more worms than the first duckling. And the third duckling found as many worms as the other two put together. All together, how many worms did all three ducklings find?

   ____

5. The third duckling kept a record of her worm-finding each day: Monday: 27, Tuesday: 24, Wednesday: 36, Thursday: 31, Friday: 37. What was the average number of worms that the duckling found?

   ____

6. In worm-finding, the fourth duckling found 8 worms on Monday. On Tuesday, he found 5 more worms than on Monday. On Wednesday, he found twice as many worms as he found on Tuesday. How many worms did he find in all?

   ____

7. Mother Duck divided up 375 seeds into 5 equal piles for herself and her 4 ducklings. She then took 12 seeds from her own pile and added them to the pile of each of her ducklings. How many seeds were now in each pile?

   Mother Duck: ________

   Duckling 1: ________

   Duckling 2: ________

   Duckling 3: ________

   Duckling 4: ________

8. Mother duck gathered up 120 worms and divided them into 5 equal piles. She gave 8 of her own worms to each of the first three ducklings. Then she took 3 of *their* worms and gave them to the fourth duckling. How many worms did each duck end up with?

   Mother Duck: ________

   Duckling 1: ________

   Duckling 2: ________

   Duckling 3: ________

   Duckling 4: ________

pages 8–9

1. 10
2. 18
3. 8
4. 3 x 6 = 18
5. 2 x 6 = 12
6. 5 x 4 = 20
7. 21
8. 16
9. 28
10. 28

page 10

1	2	3	4	5	6	7	8	9
2	4	6	8	10	12	14	16	18
3	6	9	12	15	18	21	24	27
4	8	12	16	20	24	28	32	36
5	10	15	20	25	30	35	40	45
6	12	18	24	30	36	42	48	54
7	14	21	28	35	42	49	56	63
8	16	24	32	40	48	56	64	72
9	18	27	36	45	54	63	72	81

pages 11–12

1. 4
2. 3
3. 5
4. 12 ÷ 3 = 4
5. 15 ÷ 5 = 3
6. 16 ÷ 4 = 4
7. 8
8. 5
9. 4
10. 6

page 13

1	2	3	4	5	6	7	8	9
1	2	3	4	5	6	7	8	9
1	2	3	4	5	6	7	8	9
1	2	3	4	5	6	7	8	9
1	2	3	4	5	6	7	8	9
1	2	3	4	5	6	7	8	9
1	2	3	4	5	6	7	8	9
1	2	3	4	5	6	7	8	9
1	2	3	4	5	6	7	8	9

page 15

1. 8 x 3 = 24 clients
2. 9 x 6 = 54 hours
3. 4 x $8 = $32
4. 8 x 9 = 72 ads
5. $8 million x 3 = $24 million, $6 million x 4 = $24 million, $24 million + $24 million = $48 million
6. $7 + $3 = $10, $10 x $5 = $50
7. $5 + $2 = $7, $7 x $5 = $35, $50 - $35 = $15
8. Roaring 7 times for $8 per roar is more. It is $2 more.

pages 16–17

1. 16 ÷ 4 = 4 yards
2. 27 ÷ 3 = 9 yards
3. 48 ÷ 6 = 8 seconds
4. 42 ÷ 6 = 7 pushups each day
5. 63 ÷ 7 = 9 sit-ups
6. 24 ÷ 4 = 6 minutes
7. 20 ÷ 4 = 5 yards
8. 72 ÷ 9 = 8 seconds
9. 24 ÷ 2 = 12; 24 ÷ 3 = 8; 24 ÷ 4 = 6; 24 ÷ 6 = 4; 24 ÷ 8 = 3; 24 ÷ 12 = 2

page 19

1. 8 x 6 = 48 ounces
2. 9 x 6 = 54 ducats
3. 4 x 6 = 24 ducats, 5 x 7 = 35 ducats, 24 + 35 = 59 ducats
4. 100 - 40 = 60, 60 ÷ 6 = 10 months
5. 60 ÷ 5 = 12 months
6. 100 ÷ 4 = 25 bowls
7. 3 x 3 = 9, 9 x 9 = 81 ducats
8. 120 - 48 = 72, 72 ÷ 8 = 9 pages
9. 75 - 41 = 34, 34 + 22 = 56, 56 ÷ 7 = 8 weeks

pages 20–21

1. 210
2. 280
3. 40
4. 60
5. 80
6. 120
7. 120
8. 240
9. 200
10. 480
11. 1600
12. 4000
13. 500
14. 700
15. 1500
16. 1400
17. 2000
18. 8000
19. 80,000
20. 20,000
21. 300,000
22. 1,500,000; attached five zeroes

page 23

1. 60
2. 70
3. 30
4. 70
5. 60
6. 40
7. 60
8. 70
9. 80
10. 40
11. 600
12. 500
13. 700
14. 800
15. 400
16. 900
17. 900
18. 600
19. 10,000
20. 6; attached one less zero to the quotient.

pages 24–25

1. 360
2. 70 x 6 = 420
3. 120
4. 120
5. 250
6. 120
7. 180
8. 490
9. 400
10. 1200
11. 80 x 40 = 3200
12. 90 x 60 = 5400
13. 300
14. 600
15. 2500

16. 3500
17. 20 x 30 = 600 pages
18. $30 x 60 = $1800

pages 26–27

1. 30
2. 30
3. 70
4. 320 ÷ 8 = 40
5. 20
6. 10
7. 80
8. 90
9. 80
10. 80
11. 70
12. 90
(possible answers are given)
13. 250 ÷ 5 = 50
14. 360 ÷ 6 = 60
15. 25
16. 80
17. 40
18. 70
19. 450 ÷ 90 = 5
20. 2
21. 5
22. 9

pages 28–29

1. 56
2. 108
3. 172
4. 105
5. 371
6. 360
7. 282
8. 322
9. 624
10. 445
11. 2932
12. 2415
13. 3756
14. 4088
15. 5370
16. 3573
17. 2190 days
18. 2856 ducats

page 31

1. 1104
2. 1575
3. 2774
4. 3318
5. 1170
6. 455
7. 1512
8. 1752
9. 1188
10. 2064
11. 1798 ducats
12. Estimate should be 4000. Rolvar's answer is too high.

pages 32–33

1. 13
2. 12
3. 11
4. 19
5. 31
6. 39
7. 16
8. 14
9. 73
10. 42
11. 37
12. 33
13. 24
14. 45
15. 57
16. 36

pages 34–35

1. 9912
2. 9159
3. 4880
4. 11,802
5. 22,505
6. 13,946
7. 32,618
8. 67,991
9. 216,810
10. 266,630
11. 310,245
12. 82,656
13. 279,174
14. 350,448
15. 778,872
16. 690,562

pages 36–37

1. 25 R 2
2. 29 R 1
3. 18 R 3
4. 32 R 5
5. 284 R 2
6. 114 R 2
7. 93 R 3
8. 49 R 1
9. 115 R 1
10. 94 R 3
11. 23 per customer, 3 minutes left over
12. 28 customers

pages 38–39

1. 18
2. 5
3. 14
4. 13
5. 32 R 5
6. 4 R 32
7. 21
8. 36
9. 17
10. 20
11. 27
12. 31

pages 40–41

(answers are rounded to the nearest whole)
1. $126 ÷ 9 = $14
2. $1253 ÷ 9 = $139
3. $1253 - $126 = $1127
4. $1127 ÷ 9 = $125
5. $126 ÷ 9 = $14, $14 ÷ 7 = $2
6. 18 x $36 = $648
7. bad deal, $702 - $648 = $54
8. 35 x $171 = $5985,
13 x $126 = $1638,
$5985 +$1638 = $7623

pages 42–43

1. $4.90
2. $16.90
3. $2.10
4. $121.90
5. $3417.50
6. 53.1

7. $650
8. 2463
9. 7.6
10. $4512
11. 637
12. 6522
13. 170.9
14. $5612
15. 5254
16. 1439
17. 43 ounces
18. $47

pages 44–45

1. $0.88
2. 4.431
3. 16.81
4. 0.55
5. 1.11878
6. $0.62
7. 2.556
8. 82.574
9. $7.83
10. 91.23
11. 0.6522
12. 4.4167
13. 0.2943
14. 87.23
15. 6.622
16. 0.059
17. $8759 ÷ 10 = $875.90
18. $8759 ÷ 100 = $87.59

pages 46–47

1. 10.2
2. 12.6
3. 1.96
4. 157.08
5. 1754.4
6. 144.50
7. 22.79
8. 555.45
9. 2502.9
10. 37.26
11. 6674.8
12. 1711.5
13. 5.75
14. 8.32
15. 0.042
16. 12.121

pages 48–49

1. 8.4
2. 4.6
3. 13.1
4. 19.4
5. 1.77
6. 0.72
7. 28.32
8. 3.87
9. 0.493
10. 0.468
11. 1.321
12. 0.238
13. 0.443
14. 0.0845

pages 50–51

1. 2
2. 7
3. 2
4. 4
5. 8
6. 4
7. 9
8. 4
9. 18
10. 25
11. 12
12. $\frac{15}{2}$
13. $\frac{1}{4}$
14. $\frac{1}{6}$
15. $\frac{3}{32}$
16. $\frac{3}{8}$
17. $\frac{2}{5}$
18. $\frac{2}{7}$
19. $\frac{1}{6}$
20. $\frac{4}{7}$

page 53

1. 13 x 7 = 91, 91 ÷ 30 = 3; 1 ounce left over
2. 13 x 7 = 91, 6 x 7 = 42, 91 + 42 = 133, 133 ÷ 30 = 4 jugs; 13 ounces left over; 1 guest can have a third glass
3. 23 x 8 = 184, 184 ÷ 30 = 6 jugs (4 ounces left over)
4. Rowena should buy six 9-foot panels totaling $118 and two 3-foot panels totaling $10, for a grand total of $128.
5. If Rowena cuts panels down to size, she should buy three 28-foot panels for a total of $73.50. She will have 6 feet left over.

page 55

1. 612.9 feet
2. 1089.68 sq ft
3. 31.8 feet
4. 817.26 sq ft
5. 151.6 feet
6. 1374 sq ft
7. 16.8 feet
8. 14 feet
9. 8 feet
10. 90 feet

page 57

1. 179.9699
2. 25
3. 10
4. 336.9248
5. 2339.3286
6. 6696.84
7. 0.31325
8. 0.7553844 ounces
9. 1.11984 ounces
10. 8517 miles wide
11. 33.8959 degrees

page 59

1. 32
2. 32 seconds
3. 14 yards per second
4. 130 worms altogether
5. 31 worms
6. 39 worms
7. Mother Duck: 23, Duckling 1: 87, Duckling 2: 87, Duckling 3: 87, Duckling 4: 87
8. Mother Duck: 0, Duckling 1: 29, Duckling 2: 29, Duckling 3: 29, Duckling 4: 33

Notes

Notes